The Age of
Diminished Expectations

The Age of
Diminished Expectations

U.S. Economic Policy
in the 1990s

Paul Krugman

The MIT Press
Cambridge, Massachusetts
London, England

This book was originally published as a *Washington Post Company Briefing Book.*

This book was set in Palatino by The MIT Press. It was printed and bound in the United States of America.

Library of Congress Cataloging-in-Publication Data

Krugman, Paul R.
   The age of diminshed expectations: U.S. economic policy in the 1990s /
Paul Krugman.
     p. cm.
   Includes index.
   ISBN 0-262-11156-X.
   1. United States—Economic policy—1981– 2. Economic forecasting—United
States. I. Title.
HC106.8.K78 1990
338.973'001—dc20   90-6310
                                           CIP

Contents

Foreword by Paul A. Samuelson   vii
Preface   ix

Introduction   1

I   The Roots of Economic Welfare

1   Productivity Growth   9

2   Income Distribution   19

3   Employment & Unemployment   27

II   Chronic Aches & Pains

4   The Trade Deficit   35

5   Inflation   51

III   Policy Problems

6   The Budget Deficit   63

7   The Triumphant Fed   79

8   The Dollar   89

9   Free Trade & Protectionism   101

10   Japan   115

IV Financial Follies

11   The Savings & Loan Scandal   135

12   Third World Debt   143

13   Corporate Finance   153

V American Prospects

14   Happy Ending   171

15   Hard Landing   177

16   Drift   191

Index   199

Foreword

Today economic writing is better than ever it used to be. But now there is so much of it—often arguing at cross-purposes—that you as an intelligent and motivated reader are more up in the air than ever. What to do?

Needed is a competent guide, prepared by a tested and proved researcher, a briefing book to select the essentials for emphasis and sort them out in a good-sense way that will earn your confidence and understanding. That is a tall order. But Paul Krugman is the economist to try to do the job. And I see that he has succeeded wonderfully well.

I am proud of my generation of policy economists. You know their names: Walter Heller, Milton Friedman, John Kenneth Galbraith, Arthur Okun, Herbert Stein, Peter Drucker, and many more. But, as some sage has said, science progresses funeral by funeral. Paul Krugman is the rising star of this century and the next, and the world beats a path to his door. International finance is his thing, but that is only one of the many strings to his fiddle. The World Bank, the IMF, the Bank of Japan, and the Boston Fed—all seek to tap his fountain of wisdom and new ideas.

The Age of Diminished Expectations is a tour de force. To economists and noneconomists using it as a chart to navigate through the mysteries of inflation and recession, supply-side economics and productivity, floating exchange rates and bouncing stock markets, I say *Bon Voyage*!

Paul A. Samuelson
May 1990

Preface

There are three kinds of writing in economics: Greek-letter, up-and-down, and airport.

Greek-letter writing—formal, theoretical, mathematical—is how professors communicate. Like any academic field, economics has its fair share of hacks and phonies, who use complicated language to hide the banality of their ideas; it also contains profound thinkers, who use the specialized language of the discipline as an efficient way to express deep insights. For anyone without graduate training in economics, however, even the best Greek-letter writing is completely impenetrable. (A reviewer for the *Village Voice* had the misfortune to encounter some of my own Greek-letter work; he found "equations, charts, and graphs of stunning obscurity . . . a language that makes medieval scholasticism seem accessible, even joyous.")

Up-and-down economics is what one encounters on the business pages of newspapers, or for that matter on TV. It is preoccupied with the latest news and the latest numbers, hence its name: "According to the latest statistics, housing starts are up, indicating unexpected strength in the economy. Bond prices fell on the news . . . " This kind of economics has a reputation for being stupefyingly boring, a reputation that is almost entirely justified. There is an art to doing it well—there is a Zen of everything, even short-term economic forecasting. But it is unfortunate that most people think that up-and-down economics is what economists do.

Finally, airport economics is the language of economics best-sellers. These books are most prominently displayed at airport bookstores, where the delayed business traveler is likely to buy them. Most of these books predict disaster: a new great depression, the evisceration of our economy by Japanese multinationals, the collapse of our money. A minority have the opposite view, a boundless optimism: new technology or supply-side economics is about to lead us into an era of unprecedented economic progress. Whether pessimistic or optimistic, airport economics is usually fun, rarely well informed, and never serious.

But what is there for the intelligent reader who wants to be well informed but doesn't want to study for a Ph.D.? The answer, unfortunately, is not much.

In 1989 the *Washington Post* approached me with the idea of writing a short book about the U.S. economy that would be accessible to a nonprofessional public while maintaining intellectual quality. They envisioned this as a pilot for a series of briefing books on a variety of issues, from national defense to the environment, where the specialists and the educated public had ceased to speak a mutually intelligible language. This book is the result.

The title of the book, and its theme, came to me when I tried to put my finger on what airport economics gets wrong. The most important problem with the books at the newsstand, it seemed to me, is that they allow no middle ground between disaster and bliss. Either the economy is about to disintegrate or things will be wonderful—and since the economy rarely disintegrates, those people who are not in a doom-and-gloom mood will usually conclude that we are doing fine. Yet avoiding crisis and doing well are not the same thing.

The simple fact is that the U.S. economy is not doing well, compared with any previous expectation. In the late 1960s, nearly everyone expected the great postwar boom to continue. *Fortune*, for example, predicted in 1967 that real wages would increase by 150 percent by the year 2000. In fact, real wages are no higher now than they were at the time of the article. While a few Americans have prospered to an unprecedented extent, poverty in America has been increasing in both extent and severity. A persistent trade deficit has accelerated America's relative decline in the world economy, to the point where we may well be the third-ranked economic power by the end of this decade.

When will these disappointments come to a head? Quite possibly never—which is why airport economics is so misleading. One can have stability without progress, avoid a depression without achieving sustained economic growth. That has been the basic story of the U.S. economy since the early 1970s, and will probably be its story for the 1990s.

One might have expected that America's economic problems would have come to a head in another way, through the political process. Relative to what almost everyone expected twenty years ago, our economy has done terribly; surely one should have expected a drastic political reaction. I find the lack of protest over our basically dreary economic record the most remarkable fact about America today. Whether it is a sign of our political strength or weakness, it is astonishing how readily Americans have scaled down their expectations in line with their performance, to such an extent that from a political point of view our economic management appears to be a huge success.

This, then, is my theme. We live in an "age of diminished expectations," an era in which our economy has not delivered very much but in which there is little political demand that it do better.

In this book I try to document both our economic failures and our successes. More important, I try to explain *why* we are not making more of an effort to do something about our disappointing econ-omy—which comes down in large part to the painfulness of the measures that we would have to take if we were serious about making a difference. And I try to chart the eventual consequences of continuing our present policy.

Along the way this book tries to convey a number of things that professional economists know but that the broader public gener-ally does not. It is important to understand why inflation is less costly to endure and more costly to stop than most people realize; why protectionism, while usually a bad thing, does not cause de-pressions; how the savings-and-loan debacle was created by mis-placed free-market rhetoric. On these and other issues I have found that the simple truth is widely regarded as shocking and heretical.

I hope that America will eventually be roused from its slumber and once again begin to face up to problems instead of letting them slide. The beginning of action must, however, lie in understanding. This book is not a political tract or a call to arms. It is something rarer: an attempt to describe the way things are, and explain why.

**The Age of
Diminished Expectations**

Introduction

George Bush won the 1988 presidential election for a number of reasons, but the most important was that the U.S. economy was doing well enough to satisfy most voters. Incumbent parties almost always keep the White House if inflation is moderate and the unemployment rate is falling in the year leading up to the election. With inflation of less than 4 percent in 1988, and the economy in its sixth year of steady growth and falling unemployment, Bush was swept into office on a wave of economic contentment.

Yet at a deeper level the complacency with which the American people view their economy is something of a puzzle. Leave aside the worries about the budget and trade deficits—these are hopelessly abstract to most people, who are seldom moved by the warnings of doomsayers. It still remains true that the performance of the U.S. economy in the 1980s was disappointing by past standards. Although some people became fabulously rich, and a sizable fraction of the population achieved unprecedented affluence, the typical American family and the typical American worker earned little if any more in real terms in 1988 than they did in the late 1970s. Indeed, for the median American worker there has been no increase in real take-home pay since the first inauguration of Richard Nixon. And for Americans in the bottom fifth of the income distribution the 1980s have been little short of nightmarish, with real incomes dropping, the fraction of the population in poverty rising, and homelessness soaring.

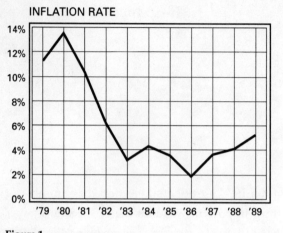

Figure 1
Inflation declined in the 1980s . . .

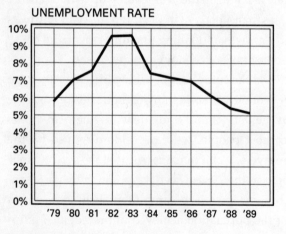

Figure 2
. . . and unemployment, after rising sharply at the beginning of the decade,
began a steady decline.

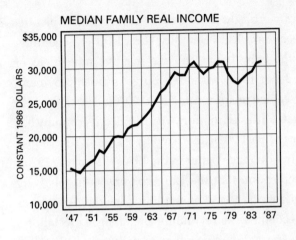

Figure 3
But the real income of typical families stagnated . . .

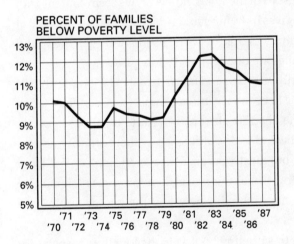

Figure 4
. . . and more people were in poverty at the end of the decade than at the beginning.

There are, of course, bright aspects to the U.S. economic picture. The American economy has been very successful at generating jobs, absorbing the baby boom and the massive movement of women into the labor force without a bulge in unemployment. Inflation, which seemed out of control in the 1970s, has subsided to a level that generates little discomfort. Yet overall our economy has done worse over the past 20 years than anyone would have predicted, and it didn't do much better in the 1980s than in the 1970s.

The general perception that the U.S. economy is in relatively good shape, then, reflects a kind of revolution in what Americans expect of their economy—a revolution of falling expectations. Americans once expected their economy to deliver steadily rising standards of living, with each generation markedly better off than its parents. At the start of the 1990s, however, we seem content with an economy that gives us living standards that creep up slowly if at all—so long as most people who want jobs can get them and inflation does not erode our paychecks too quickly.

In 1988 the Democrats tried and failed to make the long-term performance of the U.S. economy into a campaign issue. They failed partly because they had no clear idea what to do about it, partly because the public had little confidence in their capacity as economic managers, but mostly because the American people did not share their concern. The election was therefore a clear signal that economic policy has entered a new era: the age of diminished expectations.

The purpose of this briefing book is to explore the prospects for economic policy in this new age. Most tracts on the economy written in these times are exhortatory. They attempt to rouse the political system out of its complacency, to warn of the approaching crisis that looms if we don't eliminate the budget deficit, develop a strategy to compete with Japan, or whatever else is on the author's agenda. Such warnings should not be dismissed, since economic crises do happen, and it is a sure bet that America will face one sooner or later. In the current American mood, however, nobody is going to take a politically risky action just on a warning.

Since my purpose here is to ask what might actually happen, not what should happen, this book asks not what bold things the government should do, but rather where and whether crises might force policy changes despite the political system's determination to avoid trouble. After examining the specific issues that will confront economic policy, we turn to the general prospect: Will the American economy prosper despite the lack of strong policy direction, run into crises that force action, or simply drift along?

The book is divided into five parts. The first part addresses the overall economic landscape: the trends that have had the biggest impact on the well-being of large numbers of Americans. A clear view of these trends is important if we want to know how well the economy is doing—but they are not policy issues right now because no seriously debated policy changes would affect them very much.

The second part turns to two aspects of the economy that are widely regarded as problems, and that our government could resolve if it really wanted to: the trade deficit and inflation. As will become clear, however, the government in fact has balked at doing anything significant to reduce either the trade deficit or the rate of inflation—and in this age of diminished expectations, that lack of action has proved acceptable to the public, so long as no crisis results.

The third part of the book discusses a series of narrower policy issues, all interrelated: the budget deficit, monetary policy, the dollar, protectionism and U.S.-Japan relations. All of these issues bear on, and are colored by, concerns about trade and inflation.

No picture of the American economy at the beginning of the 1990s would be complete without some mention of the extraordinary changes that have taken place in the financial markets. The fourth part of the book describes three "financial follies": the savings and loan crisis, the morass of Third World debt, and the wild world of corporate finance.

The book ends with a discussion of America's prospects: What is likely to go wrong (or right) with the U.S. economy? Will the policy sins of the 1980s meet retribution in the 1990s? Will we on the contrary experience a renewed prosperity that makes the doom-sayers seem foolish? Or will we simply drift along as we have, neither doing well nor experiencing a crisis?

I   The Roots of Economic Welfare

The well-being of the economy is a lot like the well-being of an individual. My happiness depends almost entirely on a few important things, like work, love, and health, and everything else is not really worth worrying about—except that I usually can't or won't do anything to change the basic structure of my life, and so I worry about small things, like the state of my basement. For the economy, the important things—the things that affect the standard of living of large numbers of people—are productivity, income distribution, and unemployment. If these things are satisfactory, not much else can go wrong, while if they are not, nothing can go right. Yet very little of the business of economic policy is concerned with these big trends.

To many readers this list may seem too short. What about inflation or international competitiveness? What about the state of the financial markets or the budget deficit? The answer is that these problems are in a different class, mainly because they have only an indirect bearing on the nation's well-being. For example, inflation (at least at rates the United States has experienced) does little direct harm. The only reason to be concerned about it is the possibility—which is surprisingly uncertain—that it indirectly compromises productivity growth. Similarly, the budget deficit is not a problem in and of itself; we care about it because we suspect that it leads to low national saving, which ultimately leads to low productivity growth.

So it is important to start our tour of the economy with the right perspective, which is that only the big three issues really matter very much. It is also important to be aware that on two out of the three big issues the American economy has not been performing at all well. Unfortunately, as we review the state of play on these big issues, we will also see that nobody is likely to do much about them.

1 Productivity Growth

Productivity isn't everything, but in the long run it is almost everything. A country's ability to improve its standard of living over time depends almost entirely on its ability to raise its output per worker. World War II veterans came home to an economy that doubled its productivity over the next 25 years; as a result, they found themselves achieving living standards their parents had never imagined. Vietnam veterans came home to an economy that raised its productivity less than 10 percent in 15 years; as a result, they found themselves living no better—and in many cases worse—than their parents.

Although the overwhelming importance of productivity should be obvious, not everyone understands it—or worse, they think that productivity is important for the wrong reasons, such as to help our international competitiveness. So it is worth spending a little while thinking about the issue.

As a starting point, it might be useful to think about how productivity and living standards would be related if the United States did not have any foreign trade. This may seem an outrageous omission, since many people think that productivity is important precisely because we need to be productive to compete on world markets. But this isn't really right—and imagining an economy without trade is a good way to see why.

Suppose, then, that the U.S. economy has no foreign trade so that everything we consume has to be made here. (Incidentally, this isn't such a bad approximation to reality. Even in 1990, with a more integrated world economy than ever before, about 87 percent of the goods and services we consume in the United States will be produced here.) How could we raise our consumption per capita? As a matter of pure arithmetic, there are only three ways:

(i) We could increase our productivity so that each worker produces more.

(ii) We could put a larger portion of the population to work.

(iii) We could put a smaller fraction of our output aside as investment for the future and devote more of our productive capacity to manufacturing goods for current consumption.

Obviously, (iii) is not a long-term way to increase consumption: We can consume more for a while by investing less, but that will surely cut into our ability to consume later. Option (ii) can work for a while if a substantial fraction of the population is unemployed, or if social change brings new groups into the work force; thus rapid growth in the share of the population employed took place as America emerged from the Depression, and again in the 1970s as women entered the work force in large numbers. But over the long term there are evident limits on this: You can increase the share of the population employed from 57 to 62 percent, as we did in the 1970s and 1980s, but you can't increase it to 105 percent.

So the only way in which sustained, long-term growth in living standards can be achieved is by raising productivity. Real consumption per capita in the United States today is about four times what it was at the turn of the century; so is productivity.

Now let's put foreign trade back into the picture. As a trading economy the United States sends part of its output abroad as exports, while importing part of what its people consume. If we can somehow manage to import more without having to export more as well, we can also increase our consumption. This therefore adds two more ways in which per capita consumption can rise:

(iv) We can import more without selling more abroad—which means that we have to borrow or sell assets to pay for the extra imports.

(v) We can get a better price for our exports so that we can afford to import more without borrowing.

Obviously (iv), like (ii), is an option for the short term only, since eventually the borrowing needs to be repaid. As for (v), the problem is how to persuade foreigners to pay more for our goods. The only reliable way to do that is to make our goods better—which is really just a productivity increase under another name.

So the essential arithmetic says that long-term growth in living standards—like the doubling of our standard of living in the generation following World War II, or the tenfold increase in living

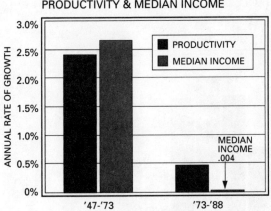

PRODUCTIVITY & MEDIAN INCOME

Figure 5
The stagnation of real family incomes during the 1970s and 1980s, like the soaring incomes of the previous generation, was driven by trends in productivity. The doubling of productivity from World War II to 1973 also doubled real incomes; the stagnation of productivity since then has held family incomes down.

standards that Japan has experienced since 1950—depends almost entirely on productivity growth.

Nor are living standards the only thing for which national productivity growth is the decisive factor. Shifts in national power are, in the end, dominated by productivity. Since World War II, productivity growth in Britain has averaged about 1.5 percent a year; in Japan it has averaged 7 percent. Britain won the war, and Japan lost; yet Britain has become a third-rank power, while Japan is on the verge of becoming a first-rank one.

In this light the slowdown of American productivity growth since the early 1970s becomes the most important single fact about our economy. Over the first 70 years of this century, American output per worker rose at an average annual rate of 2.3 percent. During the 1950s and 1960s that rate was 2.8 percent. Since 1970, however, our economy has delivered average annual productivity growth of only 1.2 percent. Had productivity over the last 20 years grown as fast as it did for the first 70 years of this century, our living standards would now be at least 25 percent higher than they are.

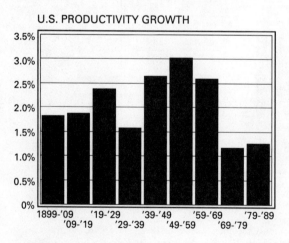

U.S. PRODUCTIVITY GROWTH

Figure 6
The two decades since 1970 have seen the worst U.S. productivity performance of the century.

Compared with the problem of slow productivity growth, all our other long-term economic concerns—foreign competition, the industrial base, lagging technology, deteriorating infrastructure, and so on—are minor issues. Or more accurately, they matter only to the extent that they may have an impact on our productivity growth.

Obviously, then, productivity must be a key political issue, right? Wrong. Economists and business managers occasionally attempt to make it an issue, but their efforts are largely ignored. Nor is this simply a matter of public ignorance. Even among the experts, be they think-tank intellectuals or academic economists, stagnant American productivity is not a fashionable topic. Of course it's important, agrees anyone who thinks about it; but there's nothing much to do about it, so why make a fuss?

This apathy among the experts becomes a little more comprehensible if we ask how economists answer two central questions about America's productivity slump: Why did it happen? And what can we do about it? The answer to both is the same: We don't know.

Start with the first question: Why did productivity growth, which did so well in the 1950s and 1960s, slow to a crawl thereafter?

A decade ago, when the productivity slowdown was still a new event, many people thought that it could be attributed to the energy crisis. The timing was right: The productivity slowdown first became apparent in the five years following the worldwide oil crisis of 1973. This theory was reinforced by the fact that productivity slowed everywhere, not just in the United States. Indeed, the slowdown in West Germany and Japan was even greater than in America (although growth was faster in both countries both before and after the slowdown).

Many economists were never happy with the energy crisis explanation of the productivity slowdown, for a variety of technical reasons. But that technical debate has now become moot: In the 1980s energy prices fell sharply—in real terms almost back to their 1973 levels. If the energy crisis of the 1970s caused the productivity slump, then the reverse energy crisis of the 1980s should have spurred a corresponding productivity boom. It didn't.

This left economists with a set of explanations for the productivity slump that are little more than sophisticated cocktail party chatter. Conservative economists predictably place the blame on increased government regulation—yet productivity growth has been higher in the highly regulated economies of Western Europe than in the United States, and America's move to deregulation in the 1980s has not borne fruit in any re-acceleration of growth.

Other economists point to the long-term effects of the social upheavals of the 1960s on mores, motivation, and the quality of education—what might be called "the *thirtysomething* theory"—though this is not what you call serious economic analysis. As MIT economist Robert Solow has put it, most discussions of poor productivity performance end in "a blaze of amateur sociology."

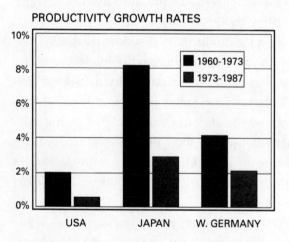

Figure 7
Productivity growth slowed around the world in the early 1970s.

So we really don't know why productivity growth ground to a near-halt. That makes it hard to answer the other question: What can we do to speed it up?

There is a standard economist's answer. Unfortunately, it is fairly depressing. If you want more output, say the economists, provide more inputs. Give your workers more capital to work with, and better education, and they will be more productive. And how are we to do these things? Simple: Suffer. Consume less now, so that more resources are available for investment. Send your children to school for more hours, and pay for the extra teachers and classrooms this requires. Do these things, and though you may be worse off right now, eventually they will pay off and living standards will rise. Ten years from now—or is it 20?—our productivity will be sufficiently higher to make up for present sacrifices.

This is not an answer that inspires fervent political support—especially when one bears in mind that the causes of the productivity slump are not obviously tied to declining investment in plant and equipment or in education. In fact, the American economy placed about as high a share of its resources into investment, and a higher share into education, in the 1970s and 1980s as it did in the 1950s and 1960s. It just didn't work as well. So the orthodox prescription for accelerating productivity growth calls on us to make unprecedented efforts, which will depress our living standards in the short run, to offset an undiagnosed ailment. This is the kind of grim advice that has caused economics to be called "the dismal science."

Can't economists think of anything more cheerful to propose? In the late 1970s, when the productivity slowdown was still news, the question of how to get growth going again called forth enthusiastic advocates of a variety of schemes. The most popular nostrums generally separated along left-right lines. On the left, there were the advocates of "industrial policy": people like Robert Reich and Lester Thurow, who thought that by playing a more active role in the marketplace, the government could accelerate productivity growth. On the right, there were supply-siders: people like Arthur Laffer and Jude Wanniski, who believed that getting the government *out* of the marketplace would unleash a wave of private sector dynamism. Although these groups were at opposite ends of the political spectrum, they had much in common. They were outside the academic mainstream, being either economic heretics like Thurow or Laffer, or noneconomists like Reich (a lawyer) or Wanniski (a journalist). And they offered the political system alternatives to the dreary virtue preached by the economics establishment. They offered free lunches—a chance to invigorate the economy without pain.

When Ronald Reagan was elected, the supply-siders got a chance to try out their ideas. Unfortunately, they failed. It was not an abject failure that left the economy in ruins—the American economy clearly did well enough in the 1980s to satisfy most voters. While there are some economists who think that the policies of the Reagan years have stored up disaster for America's future, such predictions of doom carry little political weight. But what supply-side economics in power actually delivered was so far short of what it promised that all the fire went out of the movement. The Republicans won the 1988 election, but the supply-siders were not part of the victory party. Bush's economic team consists of what the English call "Tory wets": Although they are nominally free-market conservatives, they are unwilling to contemplate further radical surgery on the economy, and they have even been tempted to reregulate in such areas as the environment and financial markets.

Yet at the same time the apostles of industrial policy have also lost much of their following. The pervasive distrust of government that spread across America in the 1980s provides a poor climate for policies that would place large discretionary power in the hands of bureaucrats. Some limited moves that one could call "industrial policy" are likely to happen over the next few years. Government support for semiconductors is already a modest reality; high-definition television ultimately may get funds as well. But these initiatives will be marginal in scale. The political system simply has no appetite for a major experiment in industrial policy.

So what are we going to do about productivity growth in the United States? Nothing.

Well, not exactly nothing. There are various things the government can do that might accelerate productivity growth without great political risks, from encouraging higher educational standards to supporting a few industry research consortia. These things will be tried, and some of them may even work a little. But the basic political consensus at present is that a low rate of productivity growth is something America can live with.

This, then, is our first big issue. Productivity growth is the single most important factor affecting our economic well-being. But it is not a policy issue, because we are not going to do anything about it.

2   Income Distribution

Although the typical American family had about the same real income in 1988 as it did in 1978, this was not true of untypical families: the rich and the poor. The best-selling novel of 1988, Tom Wolfe's *Bonfire of the Vanities*, portrayed an America of growing wealth at the top, a struggle to make ends meet in the middle, and growing misery at the bottom. The numbers bear him out. During the 1980s the rich, and for that matter the upper middle class, became a great deal richer, while the poor became significantly poorer.

In making this comparison, it is important to be careful about starting dates. The great bulk of the population is better off now than it was in the last year of the Carter Administration or the first two years of the Reagan Administration, when the economy was in a deep recession. That recession, however, was transitory—as we will see later, it was part of a deliberate, bipartisan policy of temporarily raising unemployment in order to reduce inflation. The recession years, therefore, provide a misleading base for comparison. The more appropriate comparison is with a time of more "normal" unemployment, which puts us back to 1979. When one does this, the growth in inequality is startling.

One recent study concludes that, after adjusting for changes in family size, the real income before taxes of the average family in the top 10 percent of the population rose by 21 percent from 1979 to 1987, while that of the bottom 10 percent *fell* by 12 percent. If one bears in mind that tax rates for the well-off generally fell in the Reagan years, while noncash benefits for the poor, like public housing, became increasingly scarce, one sees a picture of simultaneous growth in wealth and poverty unprecedented in the twentieth century. The same study estimates that the fraction of Americans who are "rich" (defined by an arbitrary but constant standard) nearly doubled from 1979 to 1987, even while the fraction of families defined by the U.S. government as living in poverty simultaneously increased by 15 percent.

Even these numbers probably fail to capture the full extent of what has happened, because they miss the real extremes. The ranks of the extremely well-off were reinforced by the vast fortunes made by traders and investment bankers on Wall Street and by huge increases in executive compensation. Meanwhile, the amount of sheer misery in America has surely increased much faster than the official poverty rate, as homelessness and drug addiction have spread.

Long-term comparisons of income distribution are fraught with difficulties, but for what it is worth, standard calculations show that the surge in inequality in the United States after 1979 reversed three decades of growing equality, pushing the income shares of the top and bottom categories to their highest and lowest levels, respectively, since 1950. Since measures of inequality in 1950 were magnified by widespread rural poverty, it is probably safe to say that income distribution within our metropolitan areas is more unequal today than at any time since the 1930s.

While some conservatives do not consider income distribution a valid issue for public concern, the changes in that distribution in the 1980s had a far more important effect on people's lives than any deliberate government action. After all, even a disastrous policy blunder is unlikely to lower the real incomes of 25 million Americans by more than 10 percent; yet that is what happened to the poorest tenth of the population during the 1980s. Not everyone agrees that the soaring inequality of the 1980s was a bad thing, but it is a simple fact that the growth of both affluence and poverty in the 1980s largely reflected changes in the distribution of income, rather than in its overall level.

There are at least two reasons for arguing that the increased inequality of the 1980s changed *overall* welfare for the worse. First, most Americans do care at least a little bit about how well-off others are, and it is hard to argue with the conclusion that an extra thousand dollars of income matters more to a poor family than to someone whose income is already in six digits. Second, the income distribution colors the whole tone of society: A society with few extremes of wealth or poverty is a different, and surely more attractive, place than one with a yawning gulf between rich and poor.

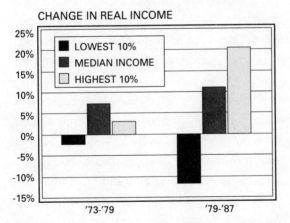

Figure 8
In the 1980s, to a much greater extent than in the 1970s, the poor got poorer while the rich got richer.

In the long run, income distribution is not as important a determinant of economic well-being as productivity growth, but in the 1980s increasing inequality in income distribution, rather than growth in productivity, was the main source of rising living standards for the top 10 percent of Americans. And the 1980s were the first decade since the 1930s in which large numbers of Americans actually suffered a serious decline in living standards.

Yet income distribution, like productivity growth, is not a policy issue that is on the table. This is partly because we don't fully understand why inequality soared, but mostly because any attempt to reverse its trend appears politically out of bounds.

One reason that action to limit growing income inequality in the United States is difficult is that the growth in inequality is not a simple picture. Old-line leftists, if there are any left, would like to make it a single story—the rich becoming richer by exploiting the poor. But that's just not a reasonable picture of America in the 1980s. For one thing, most of our very poor don't work, which makes it hard to exploit them. For another, the poor had so little to start with that the dollar value of the gains of the rich dwarfs that of the losses of the poor. (In constant dollars, the increase in per family income among the top tenth of the population in the 1980s was about a dozen times as large as the decline among the bottom tenth.)

To tell the story of what happened in the 1980s, it is necessary to paint a more complicated picture. At least three separate trends have combined to make our society radically less equal. To begin with, at the very bottom of the scale, the so-called "underclass" grew both more numerous and more miserable. Entirely unrelated, as far as anyone can tell, was a huge increase in the incomes of the very rich. In between, among those who work for a living, the earnings of the relatively unskilled fell while the earnings of the highly skilled rose.

Let's start with the underclass. While there is no generally accepted statistical definition of the underclass, we all know what it means: that largely nonwhite hard core of people caught in a vicious circle of poverty and social collapse. Attempts to measure the size of the underclass, like those of Isabel Sawhill at the Urban Institute, suggest that it began growing during the 1960s, and has continued to grow, perhaps at an accelerating rate, since then. In the 1960s and the 1970s, social programs were expected to cure persistent poverty; in the 1980s, they were widely accused of indirectly perpetuating it. At this point it appears that if you increase spending on the poor, they have more money; if you reduce it, they have less; otherwise, it doesn't make much difference. That is, neither generosity nor niggardliness seems to make much difference to the spread of the underclass. Conservatives argue that the welfare system has reduced incentives and contributed to the growth of the underclass; liberals respond that Reagan's cuts in social spending contributed to the growth of the underclass by making it more difficult for the poor to climb out of poverty. Both could be right. The most important causes of the growth in the underclass, however, like the sources of the productivity slowdown, lie more in the domain of sociology than of economics.

The increased incomes of the rich and very well-off present less of a puzzle than the growth of the underclass. While high incomes have been made in a variety of ways, one source stands out above all: finance. The 1980s were a golden age for financial wheeling and dealing, and the explosion of profits in financial operations has helped swell the ranks of the really rich—those earning hundreds of thousands or even millions a year.

Most Americans live between the stratosphere and the lower depths, and for them the growth in inequality has been yet a different story. First, there was the yuppie phenomenon: The rise of two-income professional couples has increased the number of families with $50,000 or more in annual income. Second, wage differentials among occupations widened: the real wages of blue-collar workers have declined fairly steadily for the past decade, and earnings of highly educated workers have risen rapidly. (The ratio of earnings of college graduates to those of high school graduates declined during the 1970s from 1.5 to 1.3, then rose to 1.8 during the 1980s.)

What we really don't know is why these phenomena have all happened now. The rise of two-income professional couples reflects the lagged effects of the women's movement, plus the aging of the baby boom generation. The surges in pay differentials and in market manipulation are more mysterious. Politics may have had something to do with it. The Reagan years provided a tolerant climate both for tough bargaining with workers and for financial wheeling and dealing. Other forces, like the decline of smokestack America and the consequent restructuring of the U.S. economy, may also have played a role.

Whatever the reasons for soaring inequality in the 1980s, what can policy do about it? In particular, can anything be done about the extremes of wealth and poverty that have emerged in the past decade?

The problem with poverty, as an issue, is that it has basically exhausted the patience of the general public. America launched its War on Poverty in the 1960s—a time of rising incomes and widespread optimism about government activism. This "war" was supposed to be social engineering, not merely charity. It was intended not simply to raise the living standards of the poor, but to help them work their way out of poverty. Yet poverty did not decline. Despite sharp increases in aid to the poor between the late 1960s and the mid-1970s, poverty remained as intractable as ever, and the underclass that is the most visible sign of poverty grew alarmingly. Today, relatively few people believe, as so many did in the 1960s, that government can do much to help the poor become more productive; all that it seems able to do is raise their standard of living by giving them more money (and influential books, like Charles Murray's *Losing Ground*, deny even that).

But if aid to the poor is simply charity, then its political base is nothing more than public generosity. In a time of budget deficits and largely static living standards for the average American, such generosity does not come easily. There are some modest signs of a resurgence of social activism; money may eventually become available to deal with the conspicuous poverty of the homeless; and Congress has made an effort to reform the tax system to help the working poor. But any systematic initiative to raise the incomes of the poor seems unlikely for many years.

As for the rich, a few public policy initiatives might cut down on some of their sources of income. For example, tighter regulation of financial markets might limit the number of people with incomes in the tens of millions, and a cooled-off financial market might indirectly put some limits on executive pay. For the most part, however, the only way to make the rich less so is to tax them. Yet this conflicts, or is perceived to conflict, with other policy goals—such as encouraging risk taking and entrepreneurship. Given that the deepest problem with the U.S. economy is slow productivity growth, it is difficult to argue for tax increases that might reduce incentives, even if some people make large sums in return for dubious contributions. In effect, there seems to be a public consensus that Donald Trump is the price of progress.

So income distribution, like productivity growth, is a policy issue with no real policy debate. The growing gap between rich and poor was arguably the central fact about economic life in America in the 1980s. But no policy changes now under discussion seem likely to narrow this gap significantly.

3

Employment & Unemployment

In 1989 only 5.3 percent of the work force was unemployed. This was a slightly lower rate of unemployment than in 1978 (6.0 percent), and somewhat higher than in 1970 (4.8 percent). That may not sound impressive, but in fact it was a remarkable achievement. During the 1970s and 1980s huge numbers of workers entered the U.S. labor force—baby boomers, women, immigrants. The American economy found jobs for almost all of them.

America's success in creating jobs stands out especially well when contrasted with the experience of other countries. In Europe, in particular, virtually no new jobs were created between 1973 and 1985. So even though Europe's labor force grew much more slowly than America's, unemployment increased fivefold.

Why does unemployment matter? Partly because high unemployment means that potentially productive workers are not being used, preventing the economy from producing as much as it might; partly because high unemployment breeds persistent poverty. Beyond this, however, the availability of jobs plays a key role in the way our society hangs together. A society in which young people can routinely expect to get jobs on leaving school, and to remain gainfully employed except for occasional spells for their adult lives, is going to be a very different place from one in which work is a privilege that is unavailable to many people—even if the welfare state is generous to the unemployed, as it is in much of Europe. It is a value judgment to say that a working society, other things equal, is a better society, but it is a value judgment that most Americans would share.

If unemployment is such a bad thing, then, why does the United States content itself with 5 percent or more instead of trying for something lower—say, Sweden's 3 percent, which would add more than two million additional jobs? The answer is not what you might think. It is not that there is insufficient demand for the services of unemployed workers. Creating demand for workers is not a problem for the U.S. economy: The Federal Reserve Board can create as much demand as it likes with a phone call. The problem is how to do that without also creating inflation. The principal constraint on reducing unemployment is the fear of the Federal Reserve that too low an unemployment rate will lead to accelerating inflation.

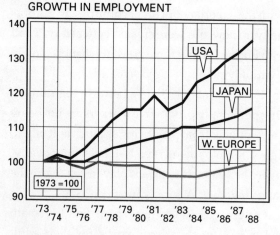

GROWTH IN EMPLOYMENT

Figure 9
U.S. employment has grown rapidly over the past 15 years; this is in sharp contrast to the experience elsewhere, especially in Europe.

Since the late 1960s, when Milton Friedman and a number of other economists proposed the concept, most economists have agreed that at any given time there is a certain level of unemployment that is consistent with stable inflation. If the government tries to increase demand to drive unemployment below that rate, it will pay the price of accelerating inflation. If the government wants to reduce the inflation rate, it must reduce demand so as to drive unemployment above this rate. The critical rate of unemployment was dubbed by Friedman the "natural rate"; other economists, disliking the suggestion that there was something good about joblessness, have proposed the alternative "nonaccelerating inflation rate of unemployment," or NAIRU.

The logic behind the idea of a NAIRU may be seen by considering the example of an economy where the government is trying to provide very full employment by keeping demand high.

Suppose that when the government starts its program of stimulus, the economy has a history of more or less stable prices. Once demand is increased, however, so that most factories run at capacity and nearly everyone can get a job, there will be a strong tendency for prices to rise. In such an economy firms will feel free to raise prices, and workers will demand wage increases over and above their rate of productivity growth. So in attempting to lower the unemployment rate from, say, 6 to 3 percent, the government might find that its formerly stable prices give way to an inflation rate of, say, 5 percent.

Now maybe the government is willing to make this trade-off. Perhaps it regards 6 percent unemployment as a much more serious problem than 5 percent inflation. Unfortunately, what it will soon find is that the trade-off is not stable. The reason is that persistent inflation gets built into people's expectations. After a few years of 5 percent inflation, workers will come to expect this inflation to continue and will make demands for wage increases over and above it. Firms will set prices higher based on the expectation that their costs and the prices of their competitors will rise at a 5 percent rate until their next price revision. And the government will find that to keep unemployment at 3 percent, it needs to accept, not 5 percent inflation, but 10 percent.

If the government still thinks the trade-off is worthwhile, then after a few more years it will find the necessary rate of inflation to be 15 percent—and so on. In the end, the only way to keep unemployment very low will be to accept an ever-accelerating inflation rate. And while 5 percent or even 10 percent inflation may be acceptable, 100 percent or 1,000,000 percent are not.

So to avoid ever-accelerating inflation, the government must accept an unemployment rate that is sufficiently high that workers do not on average demand real wage increases that exceed their productivity growth, and firms do not try to raise their prices faster than their costs. The minimum unemployment rate that will restrain inflation is the NAIRU.

The NAIRU is not an immutable, unchanging feature of the economy. Changes in long-term government policies and in the economy's structure can raise or lower it. For example, restrictive government policies that make it costly for firms to add employees can raise the NAIRU. Many economists blame such policies for "Eurosclerosis"—the persistent rise in European unemployment rates during the period 1970–1985. Demographic changes may also matter: Young workers characteristically have high unemployment rates, so an aging of the work force may lower the NAIRU. The important point, however, is that whatever the NAIRU happens to be at any given time, it places an obstacle to any attempt to expand employment by increasing demand.

Most estimates of the NAIRU for the United States currently place it somewhere between 5 percent and 7 percent. Figure 10 shows an illustration of how these estimates are made. On the vertical axis is the *change* in the rate of increase in consumer prices— for instance, if inflation goes from 3 percent to 5 percent, we indicate this as a value of +2. On the horizontal axis is the rate of unemployment. The scatter of points represents America's experience between 1973 and 1989, with each point representing a particular year. The relationship is not a particularly neat one—this is economics, not physics—but on the whole we see that inflation tended to rise when the unemployment rate was low, to fall when it was high. Notice in particular the points corresponding to the early 1980s, when very high unemployment helped bring a significant reduction in the inflation rate; these points will play a key role in the story when we examine inflation later.

A line plotted through these points crosses zero at about 6.6 percent unemployment; thus, based on the historical record, we would expect that an unemployment rate of less than 6 percent would be associated with accelerating inflation. In fact the unemployment rate in the past two years has been closer to 5 percent than

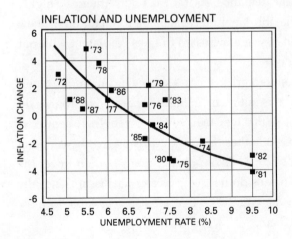

Figure 10
Inflation tends to rise when the unemployment rate is low, to fall when the unemployment rate is high.

to 6 percent, with at best a slight increase in inflation. This is reflected in the fact that the points corresponding to 1987 and 1988 lie below the line plotted in Figure 10. This may reflect a downward shift in the NAIRU—as baby boomers have become older and women more experienced, the amount of "frictional" unemployment may have declined—or it may just represent luck in what is after all an imprecise relationship.

The important point is that for the United States the NAIRU seems to have been fairly stable, or even falling, during the 1970s and 1980s. This means that there was no long-term tendency for the unemployment rate to increase—and that is quite a tribute to the adaptive ability of the American economy. As we have seen, unemployment rates in Europe rose inexorably for most of the 1970s and 1980s. The U.S. economy might easily have had big problems creating enough jobs for the enormous number of women and baby boomers who entered its labor force over the past decade. With productivity growth so sluggish, and real earnings per worker stagnant or declining, one might have expected worker frustration to lead to large wage demands. As it turned out, America's highly competitive and flexible labor markets made room for all the new entrants and limited wage increases to rates consistent with our slow productivity growth.

So unemployment is a great success story. Of course, 5 to 6 percent unemployment is not zero. Shouldn't there be a program to reduce the NAIRU, so that we can have 4 percent or less unemployment? Well, maybe—but there is no widespread agreement among economists about what kinds of policies, if any, would lower the NAIRU. And politicians do not see it as a crucial issue, since the general feeling in the country is that jobs are available to most people who want them.

II Chronic Aches & Pains

If you want to ask what really matters for the economic welfare of large numbers of Americans, productivity, income distribution, and employment are probably 90 percent of the story. If you ask what motivates actual legislation and Administration initiatives, however, these issues are probably less than 5 percent of the agenda. The reason is not that policymakers don't appreciate the importance of these central issues; it is that they see little within the normal range of policy that they can do about them. Any serious effort to increase productivity growth, or to reverse the sharp increase in income inequality, or to restructure our labor markets to get closer to true full employment, would take a degree of boldness that is rare in economic policy. Attempts to change the economic system in a fundamental way, like Franklin Roosevelt's (or Ronald Reagan's), occur only in the face of economic crisis. And while there are good reasons not to be completely happy about America's economy as the 1990s begin, it isn't in crisis—so the big issues don't move actual policy.

But the fact that the most important economic issues are, in effect, out of range does not mean that economic policymaking comes to a halt. It just means that debate focuses on issues that, while less important than, say, productivity growth, are closer to the level that might be a subject of real policy. The issues discussed in the next two chapters, while still not the direct object of legislation, are nevertheless close enough to the ground that current policy discussions are directly affected by the desire to do something about them.

There isn't as much inevitability in the choice of policy problems to discuss as there is in the case of the big issues. A decade ago, energy policy would surely have made the list; today it has faded as a major concern. A decade from now, environmental economics may well be on the list. Right now, however, the two most obvious policy problems to discuss are the trade deficit and inflation.

On these issues, as with the big issues, America's performance has been mixed. The 1980s have seen soaring trade deficits, but an impressive if not total victory over inflation. If one takes the long view, however, what is most striking about American attitudes toward economic policy is the same thing that is striking about economic performance in general: the willingness to settle for less. If the United States really wanted sharp reductions in either the trade deficit or the inflation rate, it could achieve them. But in this era of diminished expectations, nobody expects it even to try.

4   The Trade Deficit

One day last summer I had a meeting in New York. Before leaving, I set my Sharp VCR to record a television program I would miss while away. Then I drove my Mazda to the airport, boarded an Airbus A310, and while in transit finished some notes for the meeting on my Toshiba laptop computer. My suit was made in Hong Kong, my coffee cup in Portugal. It is quite possible that my breakfast cereal was the only American-made product I encountered all morning.

This was not a surprising experience in 1989, but it would have been very unusual just ten years ago. It is sometimes hard to remember that as recently as 1981, the United States exported as large a value of manufactured goods as it imported, and it remained the world's clear leader in high technology. Until the late 1970s, U.S. aircraft and computer manufacturers had no major rivals abroad; imports of foreign automobiles and consumer goods were largely restricted to the low end of the market.

The massive trade deficits that now seem a permanent feature of the U.S. scene emerged quite quickly between 1981 and 1984. In 1981 the U.S. trade picture still looked healthy. Exports of manufactured goods more than paid for manufactured imports, while exports of agricultural goods and earnings from overseas assets more than covered the cost of oil imports. The broadest measure of

U.S. trade, the so-called current account of the balance of payments, was in modest surplus, as it had been for most of the century. By mid-1984, however, the current account was in deficit at an annual rate of more than $100 billion, and despite some recent reductions there is little prospect that it will fall below that level for years to come. (In fact, it is more likely to increase.)

Many critics of American economic policy in the 1980s point to the trade deficit as evidence that the perceived prosperity of the decade was built on sand. The general public, while sanguine about the economy generally, is worried about the trade deficit; rising public concern led to the passage of the 1988 Trade Act, a law, while not overtly protectionist, certainly carries a tougher tone than its predecessors. Yet there are also respectable voices claiming that the deficit presents no problem, or even that it is a sign of American strength. Before we even ask why the United States has begun to run a trade deficit, we need to ask why the trade deficit matters.

Why worry about the trade deficit?

Ask the man in the street why a trade deficit is a bad thing, and he will probably answer that it costs America jobs. The point seems obvious enough: If we spend more on imports than foreigners spend on our exports, the result is reduced demand for American labor. The immediate job costs of international competition are easy to understand: plants closed because of competition from imports, workers laid off because of the drying up of export markets. At first glance the numbers can seem very impressive. In 1989 the United States seemed likely to run an overall current account deficit of $130 billion, about 2.3 percent of our national income. If we could somehow keep those dollars home, spending the money on American goods, the extra demand would be enough to employ about

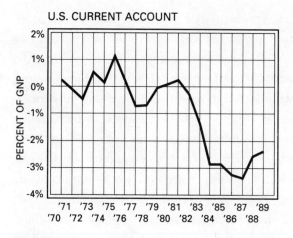

U.S. CURRENT ACCOUNT

Figure 11
The U.S. economy generally ran small surpluses on its current account, the
broadest measure of its international trade, until 1981. In the 1980s, however, the
nation plunged into a deep trade deficit. This deficit peaked in 1987 and has
declined modestly since then, especially when measured as a share of national
income.

two million more workers. It is natural to imagine that those two
million "lost jobs" are the crux of the problem.

Yet focusing on the employment effects of the trade deficit is not
only misleading—it is slightly more than 100 percent wrong.
America's trade deficit problem has nothing to do with jobs. As we
have seen, the 1980s were actually a time of quite satisfactory job
creation. New jobs created in sectors that are insulated from
international competition, such as services, far outpaced any job
losses in export or import-competing sectors. Not only did the
United States do very well at creating jobs in the 1980s despite the
ballooning trade deficit, it would have done little if any better—
indeed, probably a bit worse—had the trade deficit somehow been
prevented.

The reason is that the amount of employment offered in the U.S.
economy is ultimately limited by supply, not demand. It's easy to

increase demand: The problem is that increasing demand too much leads to inflationary pressures. Driving the unemployment rate below 5 to 6 percent will lead to accelerating inflation. Currently, U.S. unemployment is, if anything, at the low end of the safe range, so we cannot have fuller employment without higher inflation.

Imagine that America could somehow eliminate its trade deficit at a single stroke—say, by imposing quotas on imports. This would add to the current demand for labor the demand for another two million workers to fill the jobs currently "lost" because of the deficit. But would employment really rise by two million? Of course not. First of all, the United States does not have two million suitable workers available (or the plant capacity to employ them). America in 1990 is not like America in 1938, with a huge reserve army of easily employable workers ready to go to work given sufficient demand. Most of the five million or so unemployed are either unskilled or part of the inevitable "frictional" unemployment that occurs as workers change jobs or outmoded plants close. The main effect of an increase in demand would not be to increase employment but to bid up wages. To put it another way, adding two million jobs, if we could do it, would drive the U.S. unemployment rate down to around 3 percent. But that isn't possible, or at any rate not for very long: At that low an unemployment rate, inflation would begin to accelerate rapidly.

In reality, of course, that wouldn't happen. The Federal Reserve Board would raise interest rates to choke off demand and cool down the economy. Since the economy already has more or less as many workers employed as it can manage without inflationary pressure, this offset would destroy roughly as many jobs as eliminating the trade deficit would create. They wouldn't be the same jobs: Construction and service workers would be laid off while manufacturing workers were called back. But overall employment would not rise.

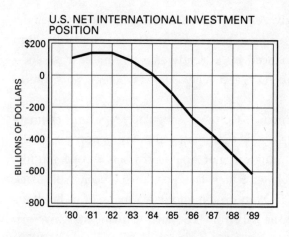

Figure 12
The trade deficits of the 1980s changed the United States from the world's largest
creditor to its largest debtor, reversing the results of 60 years of investment
abroad in only four years.

Attempts to reduce the trade deficit might even lead indirectly to
a *fall* in employment, at least for a while, as the government either
drives down the exchange value of the dollar or restricts imports,
both of which are inflationary in their own right. To keep inflation
under control would therefore take a little extra tightening on the
domestic side. So we would probably have slightly fewer jobs
without the trade deficit than we do with it.

If the trade deficit doesn't cost jobs, why worry about it? One
answer is that we shouldn't. Herbert Stein, Chairman of the President's Council of Economic Advisers under Richard Nixon, has
flatly declared the trade deficit to be a "nonproblem." A significant
minority of economists agrees with him. Some even believe that it
represents a sign of America's strength. But even these optimists
would concede that the trade deficit does have a cost: a gradual
mortgaging of future U.S. income to foreigners.

After all, the United States does not get its imports for free. When
we buy more goods and services from foreigners than we sell to

them, we must give the foreigners something else to cover the difference. What we give them is assets: The U.S. trade deficit in the 1980s was financed by a steady sale of American assets— stocks, bonds, real estate, and, increasingly, whole corporations to foreigners.

The U.S. Department of Commerce regularly reports an estimate of what it calls the U.S. net international investment position: the difference between the value of American assets abroad and foreign assets in the United States. That position has been in the black since World War I, when Britain liquidated many of its holdings here and borrowed heavily from U.S. banks to finance its war effort. The U.S. net investment position grew substantially in the 1950s and 1960s as U.S. corporations went multinational. Even during the 1970s the United States continued to invest more abroad than foreigners did here.

Our net foreign investment position reached a peak of $141 billion at the end of 1981. Then, in just four years, the result of 60 years of American overseas investment was undone. By the end of 1985, according to the Commerce Department, foreign assets in the United States exceeded American assets abroad by $112 billion. By the end of 1989 the United States was probably $650 billion in the red.

As with many of the numbers economists throw around, the net investment position is subject to some controversy. The Commerce Department measures assets at book value; this understates the true market value of most investments, but for technical reasons probably understates American assets abroad more than it understates foreign assets in the United States. So there is a case to be made that America is not as deep in the red as it appears to be, and that its transformation from creditor to debtor was a little slower— maybe we actually became a debtor country in 1987, not 1985. But no one should take comfort from this: The size of the decline is not in dispute, merely the height of the starting point.

What's wrong with being a net debtor? There is one definite cost. There are also some vaguer risks.

The definite cost is, by definition, that you owe people money. From now on, the United States will be obliged to deliver a stream of interest payments to foreign bondholders, rents to foreign land-owners, and dividends to foreign stockholders. The numbers are fairly staggering. In 1981 U.S. net investment income from abroad was $34 billion; in 1989 it was negative; and the number will continue to worsen as foreigners expand their U.S. holdings. Our payments to foreigners are a direct drain on our resources, and the longer the trade deficits continue, the larger this drain will become.

But America is a huge country; it can shrug off burdens that would crush smaller nations. The spectacular decline in our net in-vestment income since 1981, measured as a share of GNP, amounts to about a 1.5 percent drain on our economy—not a trivial number, but hardly ruinous. If the United States were to continue to sell assets at current rates, the burden of paying foreign investors could rise by an additional 2 to 3 percent of GNP by the end of the century. Again, this is serious, but no cause for panic. The United States could continue to run trade deficits as big as that of 1989 for a long time before the payment burden becomes unsupportable.

But what about the risks? The big economic risk is that as the United States becomes a massive net debtor it will be exposed to financial crises whenever the confidence of foreign investors is shaken. This is what happened to most of Latin America at the beginning of the 1980s. Banks lent the Latin nations large sums for a decade, then abruptly cut off the flow when their confidence began to waver, precipitating an economic crisis. The vision of the United States as a giant Argentina may be unlikely, but no one should dismiss it out of hand.

The other risks are political. First, there is at least some case to be made that growing foreign ownership of U.S. assets compromises our national sovereignty. We tended to dismiss this argument as patently silly when we were the foreign investors who wanted to invest in other countries. Now that the shoe is on the other foot, it seems more compelling. Second, both the trade deficit and the growing foreign stake here tend to feed crude forms of economic nationalism at home, increasing the risks of a trade war. In fact, it was primarily concern over growing protectionist pressure that led the Reagan Administration to start talking down the dollar in 1985.

The measurable costs of the trade deficit, then, are serious but not devastating. The risks are uncertain but worrisome. There isn't any reason to panic about the trade deficit, but getting it down would make everyone breathe a little easier.

But before we start talking about bringing the trade deficit down, we need to ask why we have a deficit in the first place.

Why the trade deficit?

In 1982 Martin Feldstein, the Harvard professor newly appointed Chairman of the President's Council of Economic Advisers, found a new reason to condemn the emerging budget deficit. At a time when most critics of that deficit worried that it would lead to inflation, or perhaps to high interest rates, Feldstein argued that it would lead to something quite different: unprecedented *trade* deficits. Initially his audiences were bemused. Over time, however, as the budget and trade deficits mounted together, the idea of "twin deficits" became a cliché—as well as a target for bitter attack.

Feldstein was, of course, deliberately oversimplifying. His emphasis on the linkage between the two deficits had two purposes: first, to persuade his "what-me-worry" political masters that they should do something about the budget deficit; and second, to answer protectionists who blamed the U.S. trade deficit on unfair foreign trade practices. Today, few economists believe in a simple one-to-one linkage between the budget and trade deficits. Yet a revised version of the "twin deficit" story is still the best explanation for the emergence of unprecedented trade deficits in the 1980s.

The basic story runs as follows: Beginning in 1981, U.S. national saving began to fall sharply. Only part of that fall was a result of the budget deficit—hence the need to qualify the "twin deficit" view a bit—while part of it represented a change in the behavior of households. In any case, what happened was that U.S. national saving began falling well short of U.S. investment demand, which remained strong. If the U.S. economy had not had access to world capital markets, this saving shortfall would have produced a crunch that pushed interest rates sky-high. Instead, the United States was able to turn to foreigners to fill the gap. Much of U.S. investment was financed, not out of our own savings, but through the sale of assets to foreigners.

As a matter of straightforward accounting, the United States always buys exactly as much as it sells from the rest of the world. If it sells foreigners more assets than it buys, it must correspondingly buy more goods than it sells. So the emergent U.S. dependence on foreign capital to finance its investment had as an inevitable counterpart the emergence of a trade deficit. The ultimate cause of the trade deficit therefore lies in a decline in U.S. saving—partly, but not entirely, due to the budget deficit.

Although this mainstream story is now widely accepted, many readers may feel that it is missing something. Where are all the real things that affect international trade? What happened to the dollar? What happened to U.S. competitiveness? Don't these have something to do with the trade deficit, too?

The answer is that they do, and then again at a deeper level they don't. That is, at any point in time, when we discuss the U.S. trade deficit, the level of the dollar and the international competitiveness of U.S. industry clearly matter. The ups and downs of the dollar, in particular, have been spectacular in the 1980s. When the dollar rose against the currencies of our major competitors in the first half of this decade, it sharply raised the prices of U.S. goods relative to foreign, playing a key role in encouraging imports and discouraging exports. Some of this effect was reversed when the dollar fell again after 1985. Yet even though exchange rates play a crucial role in international trade, at a deeper level capital flows are the real story.

The relationships among capital flows, exchange rates, and the U.S. trade balance have become the subject of a peculiarly nasty debate in recent years—peculiar, because the subject is relatively technical and straightforward. Yet hardly a week goes by without an angry debate between mainstream economists, who assign great importance to the exchange rate, and their critics.

One line of criticism comes from the right. Many conservatives believe that the world should return to a gold standard—that the value of each currency should be fixed in terms of gold. Since this would also fix the values of currencies in terms of each other, these conservatives are uncomfortable with the idea that changes in exchange rates may sometimes play a useful role. So they welcome the arguments of academics like Stanford's Ronald McKinnon, who declares that exchange rates are irrelevant to trade.

Other critics come from the left—people who want an active government role in promoting exports and limiting imports, and who dislike the idea that a market mechanism like the exchange rate can do the job. They therefore like the arguments of pundits such as the *New Republic*'s Robert Kuttner, who wants us to use a tough trade

WHY DEVALUATION IS SOMETIMES A GOOD IDEA

At a basic level, the United States has a trade deficit because it spends more than it earns, and Germany and Japan have trade surpluses because they earn more than they spend. That's why any attempt to solve trade imbalances simply by shifting demand from foreign to U.S. goods will fail. But if this is the case, why bother with expenditure-switching policies at all? Why is devaluing the dollar sometimes a good idea?

The reason is that trying to solve the U.S. trade deficit just by cutting U.S. spending and raising demand abroad will not lead to the right *kind* of demand. Despite the rapid increase in international trade over the past 40 years, the world economy is still far from being perfectly integrated. Most of the income of U.S. residents is spent on goods and services produced here; the same is true of Europe and Japan. As a result, most of a reduction in U.S. expenditure will be reflected, other things equal, in a fall in demand for U.S. goods and services; only a small fraction of an increase in expenditure in Europe or Japan will be spent on U.S. products.

To see the problem this causes, consider the example illustrated in the accompanying table. Imagine that the United States reduces its spending by $100 billion, while the rest of the world (ROW) simultaneously increases its demand by the same amount. Does this translate smoothly into a $100 billion reduction in the trade deficit? Unfortunately, it does not. At least $80 billion of the reduction in U.S. spending is likely to represent a fall in demand for goods and services produced here, with only $20 billion representing a fall in demand for imports. Meanwhile, no more than $10 billion of the rise in spending in the rest of the world is likely to be spent on U.S. goods, with $90 billion spent on ROW products. The result is therefore a net reduction in demand for U.S. products of $70 billion, and an equal increase in demand for ROW products. Instead of a smooth reduction in the U.S. trade deficit, we would get a combination of recession in the United States and inflation abroad. To make the adjustment work, some way has to be found to *switch* $70 billion in spending from ROW to U.S. products. The easiest way to do this is to lower the foreign exchange value of the dollar, which makes U.S. goods cheaper to ROW residents and ROW goods more expensive to U.S. residents.

The lesson of this example is that while devaluing the dollar cannot by itself solve a trade deficit, it can be crucial as part of a deficit-reduction strategy.

	Total demand	Demand for U.S. products	Demand for ROW Products
United States	−100	−80	−20
ROW	+100	+10	+90
Total	0	−70	+70

policy to bring our trade deficit down, and who accuses the advocates of a low dollar of wanting to balance trade by cutting American wages.

As usual, the intellectual debate has been warped by the political imperatives of the moment—a distortion that takes place all the more readily because it takes a little sophistication to understand what the exchange rate does and does not do.

The important thing to grasp is that the exchange rate is a crucial part of the *mechanism* that determines the trade balance, without being an independent *cause* of the trade balance. If this sounds unduly metaphysical, consider the following analogy. Think of the U.S. trade balance as an automobile. The exchange rate is not that car's engine—it is more like the drive shaft, with desired capital flows providing the motive power. In other words, changes in the exchange rate play a crucial role in translating changes in desired capital flows into changes in the trade balance, but the root cause of the trade imbalance lies elsewhere.

America's experience in the first half of the 1980s provides a good example. National saving fell—that is, consumption spending increased as a share of national income. But investment spending remained high, because an inflow of foreign capital took the place of the reduced flow of domestic saving. So overall spending in the U.S. economy rose faster than national income. The only way for an economy to spend more than it earns, however, is to import more than it exports—to run a trade deficit. So it was inevitable that the United States would develop a large trade deficit.

It was not inevitable that this trade deficit would emerge via a strong dollar. The Federal Reserve could have expanded the supply of dollars to keep the exchange rate low. But this would have led to an inflationary boom that sucked in imports (an experience that Britain has just had). As it turned out, however, the Federal Reserve kept inflation down by raising interest rates, which made dollar-denominated assets attractive to foreigners and so led to a rise of the dollar against other currencies. This rise in the dollar, by making U.S. goods expensive compared with foreign, then led to the emergence of the unprecedented trade deficits that were the counterpart of the capital inflows. The point is that while the rise of the dollar was a central part of the story as it actually played out, it is still correct to say that the U.S. trade deficit was essentially caused by the fall of national saving, which led to massive imports of capital.

What about competitiveness? It is obvious to everyone that the once-vaunted U.S. superiority over other nations in technology and quality has eroded and perhaps vanished over the past decade. Doesn't this loss of superiority help explain the rise in our trade deficit? The answer is no. If U.S. national saving had remained high, the loss of competitive advantage would not have led to a trade deficit. It would instead have led to a fall in the dollar, which would have compensated for the loss of technology and quality by making U.S. goods relatively cheaper. This is what happened in the 1970s. The United States had about the same trade balance at the end of the 1970s as it did at the beginning, but with a much lower dollar. This isn't to say that a dollar that declines every year is without costs. Competitiveness does matter—but not for the trade deficit.

We'll come back to exchange rates and competitiveness when we look at dollar policy in Chapter 8. For now, the important thing to recognize is that the root cause of the trade deficits of the 1980s was America's low national saving rate, which led it to import large quantities of capital. The next question is: What can be done about it?

Can the trade deficit be reduced?

Can the United States reduce its trade deficit? Of course it can. When it really wants to (or really has to), virtually any country can run a trade surplus. Most Latin American countries quickly shifted from large trade deficits to large trade surpluses when the debt crisis struck in the early 1980s. The United States may not want to emulate that experience, but it shows that trade deficits are not immutable facts. If America continues to run a trade deficit, it is because it chooses not to take the steps that would eliminate it.

The solution to a trade deficit has two parts. Expenditure must be both *switched* and *reduced*. Somehow people must be persuaded to switch their demand from foreign to U.S. goods—either by reducing the value of the dollar or by imposing tariffs and import quotas. But this isn't enough. There must also be a policy to reduce the level of domestic demand, so that the expenditure-switching policies don't just feed inflation.

That, of course, is the problem. We can all agree that it would be nice if Americans could sell more to foreigners and buy less, although we may argue about how best to arrange that happy event. Reducing domestic demand is another matter. Expenditure reduction hurts, and there is only one reliable way to do it: balance the Federal budget. Since the political system has no intention of doing that, there is nothing much the United States can do to eliminate its trade deficit.

It's important to understand why both switching and reducing are needed to bring down the trade deficit. Let's therefore imagine the consequences of two alternative strategies for reducing the trade deficit *without* a cut in domestic demand: an aggressive effort to drive the dollar down, making U.S. goods cheaper on world markets; and a protectionist policy that imposes new restrictions on U.S. imports.

There is no question that the government—or more accurately the Federal Reserve—could drive the dollar down if it wanted to. All it has to do is increase the supply of dollars. The resulting fall in the foreign exchange value of the dollar would certainly help U.S. exporters and make it easier for American firms to compete with imports at home.

Unfortunately, there is a side consequence of printing dollars: inflation. Any policy that tries to drive the dollar down other than by reducing our need for foreign capital will necessarily feed inflation. This is an unwanted consequence in and of itself, and it also undermines the initial objective of the policy, because inflation reduces the competitiveness of U.S. producers at any given exchange rate. The eventual result of an effort to drive the dollar down will be to raise U.S. prices by roughly the same proportion as the dollar falls, so that U.S. competitiveness is unaffected. The result, then, would be inflation with no gain on the trade front.

A protectionist policy could certainly reduce U.S. imports. But if U.S. savings have not been increased, lower imports will mean a lower supply of dollars to the foreign exchange market and thus a stronger dollar; the rise in the dollar will cut into exports and encourage increases in whichever imports are not restricted. The dollar will probably rise enough to just about eliminate the favorable impact of the import restrictions on the trade balance. The Federal Reserve could, of course, prevent the dollar from rising by printing more dollars—but this merely brings back the inflation problem.

The moral of both of these scenarios is fairly simple. There isn't much that the United States can do about its trade deficit simply by trying to encourage exports or discourage imports. The only way to cut the trade deficit successfully is to accompany export-promoting and import-cutting measures with domestic policies that reduce domestic demand—in effect making room for a trade improvement.

But how can we reduce domestic demand? For practical purposes, only one course of action is open: cutting the budget deficit. Even if you don't believe the simple "budget deficit equals trade deficit" formula that Feldstein made so popular, there are no plausible ways for the Federal government to make room for a smaller trade deficit except by balancing its budget. This might not work: Even balancing the budget might fail to reduce the trade deficit (we'll spend more time on this in Chapter 6). But it is the only plausible policy. It is also not going to happen.

So the solution to the trade deficit is both clear and unacceptable. Eliminate the budget deficit and drive the dollar down (or impose new restrictions on imports), and probably (though not certainly) the trade deficit will shrink rapidly. But since we have no intention of eliminating the budget deficit, the solution isn't available. Implicitly, the United States has decided to live with its trade deficit.

5   Inflation

The dramatic reduction in inflation in the first half of the 1980s was the great triumph of U.S. economic policy in the decade. At the end of the 1970s the U.S. inflation rate seemed out of control. In 1979, for the first time ever in peacetime, consumer prices rose at a double-digit rate (12 percent); in 1980 the inflation rate rose to 13 percent. Few would have predicted that by 1986 the inflation rate would have been just 4 percent—a rate that persisted until the decade's end.

Yet the victory was far from total. Inflation was stabilized, not eliminated, at rates that would have been regarded as unacceptable a generation ago. Public officials insist that inflation can and will be gradually eliminated. But in fact the inflation rate has changed little for the past four years. Even though inflation eased in the 1980s while the trade deficit went up, current U.S. policy toward both is much the same: to live with what we have.

Why isn't eliminating inflation a priority? For the same reasons that reducing the trade deficit isn't a priority: because the costs of living with inflation are not too high, and the costs of bringing it down look unacceptable. Given the diminished expectations of the American people, getting inflation down to the point where prices only double every 15 years is good enough.

The costs of inflation

Why is inflation a bad thing? That's a surprisingly hard question to answer. In fact, it is one of the dirty little secrets of economic analysis that even though inflation is universally regarded as a terrible scourge, most efforts to measure its costs come up with embarrassingly small numbers.

To see why, it may be useful to ask a superficially silly question: Are the British better off because they have such a valuable currency? The pound sterling is worth about $1.70 on foreign exchange markets. This means that, on average, the price rung up for any given item on an American cash register is about 1.7 times as high as the price rung up for the same item on a British cash register. Would we be better off if we made a dollar equal in value to a pound? Of course not. If the dollar were worth more, everybody's income in dollar terms would be that much less.

Now suppose that over the next ten years the overall level of U.S. prices were to rise by 70 percent (not a bad guess). Will this hurt us? Arguably it will do no more harm than deciding to use dollars instead of pounds to calculate prices. What harm does it do if all prices rise by 70 percent, if all income rises by the same amount? In real terms everyone will be in the same position, so nobody has actually lost.

That isn't the whole story, of course. But it is important to realize that to an important extent inflation is, as economists like to say, "neutral"—a general rise in prices need not affect anything real.

Where does the harm from inflation come from, then? The answer is that what really hurts the economy is not higher prices as such but the fact that prices are constantly changing, which can distort decisions and reduce the economy's efficiency.

The most concrete cost of inflation is that it discourages the use of money. In economies experiencing "hyperinflation" (that is, inflation at an annual rate in the thousands of percent), people may stop using money altogether, resorting to barter or to the use of black market foreign currency to avoid holding cash that loses value by the hour. This obviously cripples a modern economy. For an economy with inflation of 10 percent or less a year, however, the demonetizing effect of inflation is trivial.

More significant for the United States is the fact that inflation causes problems for the tax system. Inflation creates paper gains for the owners of assets that do not represent gains in real value—yet these paper gains are taxable, and so inflation may discourage saving and capital formation. On the other hand, inflation also creates paper losses for firms that have a lot of debt, which helps reduce their taxes—and it therefore encourages increased corporate debt, a phenomenon that worries many people.

Inflation may harm investment in other ways. In an inflationary world, accounting measures of corporate performance become confusing: some reported profits and losses are really just inflation illusion. Investors may therefore have difficulty evaluating firms in an inflationary world, and firms may have difficulty evaluating their own investment plans; so inflation may degrade the quality of business decisions.[1]

Lastly, unexpected inflation can produce windfall losses to individuals and institutions; even if losses are matched by gains else-

---

1. It is sometimes argued that fear of inflation discourages investment by keeping long-term interest rates high. This is half right. Expectations of inflation do keep interest rates high; but they do so precisely because borrowers are willing to pay higher rates when they expect to repay in dollars of reduced purchasing power. In fact, if we were to eliminate inflation—which would be a surprising development—the result would be catastrophic to all those firms and individuals who have borrowed long-term money at interest rates based on the assumption that inflation will reduce the real burden of repayment. So the direct effect of inflation on nominal interest rates does not systematically increase the real cost of borrowing.

where, they can be disruptive. The most dramatic example is that of the savings and loan industry, where fluctuations in the inflation rate conspired with regulatory blunders to produce a public policy disaster.

All of these costs of inflation are, however, either small or avoidable. The United States does not, at its current inflation rate, run any risk of becoming a barter economy. The tax problems caused by inflation could be met with tax reform instead of lower inflation. Accounting standards could be revised to take account of inflation. And the costs of past surprises in inflation are mostly behind us. Any future surprises will come if inflation is eliminated, not if it continues at present rates.

As far as economic analysis can tell us, a steady inflation rate of 4 or 5 percent does very little harm—and even a rate of 10 percent has only small costs.

Why, then, was a victory over inflation so important? Partly because many people *think* that inflation hurts them. The costs of higher prices on the checkout line are obvious, while the role of inflation in allowing everyone to get bigger wage increases is less so. So there may be a public perception that inflation reduces living standards even when it really doesn't.

More important, though, is the difference between a steady inflation rate and one that is accelerating. In the days of Jimmy Carter, when inflation seemed to set a new record each year, there was a widespread sense that things were out of control—this year 13 percent, next year 20 percent, maybe the year after that hyper-inflation. It was crucial to the credibility of economic policy that some kind of victory over inflation be won.

It turned out, however, that reducing inflation was not cheap. Indeed, it was almost inconceivably expensive.

The costs of disinflation

In 1980 there were many economists and politicians who thought that double-digit inflation was incurable. They were wrong. On the other hand, there were some economists, including the first Reagan Administration's advisers, who thought that victory over inflation would be cheap. They were also wrong. What happened was that the conventional *economic* wisdom, which said that reducing inflation would be very costly, proved right; but the conventional *political* wisdom, which said that these costs would never be paid, proved wrong.

How was limited victory over inflation won? Part of the answer is pure luck. In the late 1970s the inflation rate was swollen by a series of events that had little to do with economic policy. Most important, the fall of the Shah of Iran set in motion a temporary quadrupling of oil prices. Additional damage was done by soaring world food prices, driven by such disparate events as harvest failures in the Soviet Union and the disappearance of the Peruvian anchovies. In the mid-1980s, by contrast, the price of oil collapsed, and world prices of most other raw materials declined. To distinguish between these kinds of transitory events and more fundamental trends in inflation, many economists like to measure inflation, not by the change in the consumer price index per se but by looking at an "underlying" rate that leaves out changes in food and energy prices. When we look at this underlying rate, the late 1970s don't look quite as bad and the mid-1980s don't look quite as good. Still, the progress is impressive: Underlying inflation was brought down from about 10 percent in 1980 to about 4 percent in 1988.

There is no economic mystery about how this was achieved. America brought down its inflation the time-honored way: by engineering a sustained period of low output and high unemployment as a way of inducing workers to reduce their wage demands and firms to moderate their price increases. During the 1980s the United States, as a deliberate policy, put its economy through the deepest recession since the 1930s. If there is a puzzle, it is political: Why was the system willing to pay the enormous cost of this policy?

Recall the NAIRU. Any attempt to keep the unemployment rate below the NAIRU for a sustained period will lead to accelerating inflation. The converse is also true: To reduce the inflation rate, it is necessary for the economy to experience sustained unemployment rates above the NAIRU. Since a high unemployment rate corresponds to an economy running below its capacity, this means that to reduce inflation, the economy must sacrifice output.

Most estimates suggest that reducing inflation is very expensive indeed. To reduce the inflation rate by one percentage point a year, say the standard estimates, the economy has to run something like four percentage points below capacity. In another piece of ugly but useful economics jargon, this is known as the "sacrifice ratio": You have to sacrifice four points of output to reduce inflation by one point. That's a high price, even though the loss of output is only temporary while the reduction in inflation is permanent (unless you throw the gains away with irresponsible policies at a later date). It's hard to believe that anyone would be willing to pay the price of bringing the inflation rate down from 10 percent to 4 percent.

Yet that's what the United States did. Figure 13 shows the picture, which is about as clear as anything in economics. It shows two lines. One line represents "trend" output: a projection of what the U.S. economy would have produced during the 1980s if it had continued to grow steadily at the same 2.4 percent rate at which it grew from 1973 to 1979. This trend line represents a rough estimate of what the U.S. economy could have produced if it had been running

TREND vs. ACTUAL GNP

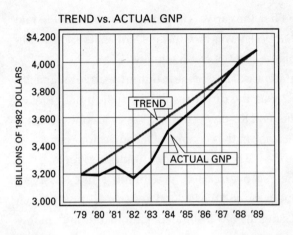

Figure 13
In the 1980s the United States followed a deliberate policy of reducing output relative to its trend, in order to reduce inflation. The cumulative "output gap," which represents the cost of our limited victory over inflation, amounted to more than 20 percent of a year's GNP.

at more or less full capacity. The other line shows the actual gross national product, which fell sharply below the trend line from 1979 to 1982, and did not get back close to the trend line until 1987. The gap between these two lines—the difference between what the economy could have produced and what it actually produced—represents a rough estimate of the cost of America's war on inflation. This gap peaked at 10 percent of GNP in 1982 and averaged 3 percent over the seven years from 1980 to 1986. That is, the U.S. economy sacrificed more than 20 percent of a year's GNP to bring inflation down. This is a huge number: 20 percent of this year's GNP would be a round trillion dollars. It is hard, in these pinched times, to imagine the U.S. government being willing to spend a trillion dollars on anything short of saving the planet, if that. Yet that was the price we paid.

There are two truths about the output gap and the war on inflation that need to be emphasized, because many people would like to deny them. First, the gap was not an accident but a deliberate policy. Second, that policy was bipartisan: Democrats and Republicans share the blame and the credit equally.

First, the deliberateness: The decline in output relative to capacity from 1979 to 1982 was the direct result of a tight money policy instituted by the Federal Reserve aimed expressly at controlling inflation by creating slack in the economy. Of course not every twist and turn was planned. There was a brief, undesired recovery in 1981, to which the Fed overreacted, precipitating an excessively deep recession. But in the end the Federal Reserve got pretty much what it wanted. Using the old-fashioned, painful, but undeniably effective medicine of recession, it brought inflation under control.

Second, the bipartisanship: The policies that produced the output gap began in 1979, under Jimmy Carter, with support from both parties. In the face of near panic over rising inflation, Carter appointed a stern central banker, Paul Volcker, as Chairman of the Federal Reserve Board, and gave him a free hand to do what was necessary. The Reagan Administration occasionally sniped at Volcker, but it too basically left him to do as he thought best. Democrats would like to blame the huge cost of the war on inflation on the Republicans; Republicans would like to blame the Democrats for the slump from ˙1979 to 1982 and take credit for the subsequent recovery. Neither party has a case.

In the end, of course, the war on inflation worked massively to the Republican party's benefit. The pain of rapidly rising unemployment came partly under Carter, and the rest came early enough in the Reagan era to be almost entirely forgotten by now. Meanwhile, the inevitable subsequent recovery of output and the lower rate of inflation helped lend a golden glow to the remaining Reagan years. This political windfall, however, reflects neither wisdom nor Machiavellianism on the part of the governing party, just luck.

What now?

The war on inflation did not end with a complete victory. Inflation has by no means been eliminated, and in 1989 it crept up again. Will there be a second war on inflation to establish full price stability?

Some people think that there should be. The reason is not that the costs of current inflation are high—even foes of inflation know that they are not. It is that if we relax about inflation it will tend to creep up, and the whole struggle will have to be repeated. For example, Herbert Stein, who dismisses the trade deficit as a "nonproblem," declares inflation to be a real problem. Why? Because "if we ... relax anti-inflation efforts now, what has been an inflation rate of 4 percent accepted on the assumption that someday we would start to get it down to zero will become a rate of 5 percent accepted on the same assumption and then 6 percent ... Someday we will have to devote ourselves to getting the rate down, and the longer we wait, and the higher the rate we start from, the more difficult and costly that will be."

On the other hand, there are economists who argue that fear of inflation, rather than inflation itself, is the real problem. Robert Eisner, a liberal economist at Northwestern University, says: "Obsessions about inflation are major obstacles, more inexcusable when the overall price level is almost stable and serious inflation clouds exist only in the minds of those for whom these are perennial fears."

Views like Stein's carry immense moral authority in Washington. In an era when conservative economic principles command more respect than they have for half a century, and with the memories of double-digit inflation still fairly fresh, few policymakers are going to declare publicly a willingness to tolerate inflation indefinitely. Officially, the Federal Reserve and the Bush Administration agree that the goal should be complete price stability within five years.

This is, however, nearly pure hypocrisy. As the experience of the 1980s shows, reducing the rate of inflation requires high unemployment. Even on an optimistic estimate, to get us from current inflation to price stability over the next five years would mean maintaining an *average* unemployment rate for the next five years of something like 7 percent, not the 5.3 percent that prevailed at the end of the 1980s. That would mean a sharp recession sometime soon—say, two years of declining GNP, driving the unemployment rate up to 8 percent—with a very slow recovery. Considering the intense criticism the Fed receives at even the hint of a mild recession, this is not likely to happen.

So the reality is that moderate inflation, like the trade deficit, has been accepted as a more or less permanent part of the American scene.

III   Policy Problems

Problems are not policies. While the trade deficit and inflation are the principal problems that worry American policymakers, actual policy is concerned with more specific questions—the budget deficit, interest rates, the dollar—that have a bearing on these problems but need to be discussed in their own right.

A description of America's economic policies is inevitably messier than a description of its problems. Policy is rarely a coherent response to perceived problems; more often it represents the outcome of bargains and struggles between groups who not only have disparate interests but also disparate perceptions of reality. It is easy to find examples of policies that seem perverse, or that work at cross-purposes. Yet the five policy issues examined here—the budget deficit, monetary policy, the dollar, trade policy, and Japan—share some underlying themes. Each issue either has, or is thought to have, something to do with the trade deficit. On each issue policy has been constrained by fear of inflation. And on each issue both policymakers and voters have proved willing to accept a level of performance that would have seemed unacceptable 15 or 20 years ago.

6   The Budget Deficit

It is easy, and perhaps appropriate, to become outraged over the persistence of the Federal deficit. Harvard economist Benjamin Friedman, in a book entitled *The Day of Reckoning*, waxes eloquent over "inaction that would have seemed unthinkable not long ago: first the pretense that there was no problem, next the wait for others to make the necessary sacrifices, and finally the complacent conclusion that nothing could be done because nothing would be done." If the apparent acceptance of more or less stagnant living standards is the most striking feature of the diminished expectations Americans have for their economy, the acceptance of a more or less permanent budget deficit is the most spectacular example of the diminished expectations the public has for its elected leaders.

Who's afraid of the deficit?

There are more than two sides to the deficit issue. Indeed, a minimum count is four, since both Democrats and Republicans are divided on the issue. On the Democratic side, one group claims that the deficit is a major problem and must be cured with a tax increase; another group claims that there is no deficit problem and new spending programs should be proposed freely. On the Republican side, one group proclaims that the deficit is a problem (though not as bad as the Democrats claim) and must be cured by cutting spending; the other claims that there is no problem, although spending should be cut anyway.

Why worry about the Federal deficit? In principle, there are two reasons. First, the government's solvency could be in danger. Second, the deficit may have negative side consequences for the economy.

The one thing clear to everyone in the deficit debate is that solvency is not a problem. The U.S. government is nowhere near being unable to pay its bills, because it can easily borrow enough to cover the deficit. Nor is the Federal debt growing fast enough to undermine this solvency anytime soon. Although the Federal debt grows at $150 billion each year, the economy and hence the Federal tax base are also growing. A useful measure of the ultimate solvency of the Federal government is the ratio of debt to gross national product. Despite years of unprecedented deficits, this number is not very different from the ratio in other countries, including Japan. Moreover, the ratio has more or less stabilized: Although Federal debt grows every year, inflation and the growth of the U.S. economy are keeping up with it. Barring an economic crisis that drastically cuts Federal revenue or pushes interest rates to unprecedented levels, the Federal government will be solvent for the foreseeable future.

So the costs of the Federal deficit are milder and more prosaic: It is alleged to drain off an important part of our national saving, leading to a low national savings rate.

Despite periodic attempts by economists to raise public concern about the problem of low national saving, neither the idea of national savings nor the reasons why it may matter have been widely appreciated. So it is worth pausing to consider what national savings are and why we should care.

RATIO OF GOVERNMENT DEBT TO GNP

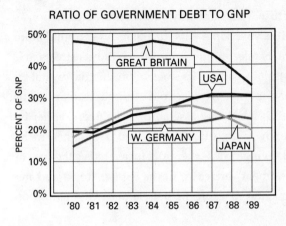

Figure 14
Despite continuing deficits, the ratio of Federal debt to GNP has stabilized at a
level not too far out of line with other industrial countries.

National savings

The discussion of national savings, like discussion of the budget
deficit itself, is a political minefield. National savings are intimately
bound up with both the budget deficit and the trade deficit, and
therefore with how you read the record of the Reagan Administration. That means that almost nobody approaches the subject without some kind of axe to grind, and that almost everyone tries to
twist the discussion in a way that reinforces his political agenda. So
it's important to start by getting the basics straight.

The first thing to get straight is that the crucial issue is *national*
savings—how much the country as a whole saves—not the savings
of any particular group inside the country. If I am convinced that
national savings are too low, and you can show me that the savings
of some particular group, like families, is fairly high, then I will not
be appeased. I will simply have to find another culprit.

The second thing to get straight is the definition of saving. Saving
means setting aside some portion of your current earnings to

provide for the future. There are only two ways that the nation as a whole can save. It can use some of its current income to build more factories, improve its telecommunications, rebuild its streets and bridges, etc. That is, it can add to its stock of productive capital by investing more than enough to replace old capital as it wears out or becomes obsolete. Or it can buy assets from foreigners, either by investing abroad or by paying off debts incurred to foreigners in the past. The national savings rate is therefore measured as the sum of net domestic investment (increases in the capital stock) and net foreign investment (increases in the net claims of the nation on foreigners).

Since the early 1980s domestic investment in the United States has been slightly lower than it was in the past. Meanwhile, America has stopped investing on net abroad and started selling huge quantities of its own assets to foreigners. So the savings of the United States as a whole were much lower in the 1980s than in the past. It's important to keep your eye on that ball. There are economists who will tell you that there really isn't any Federal deficit, if you measure it right, or that households are actually saving a lot in indirect ways, and therefore that there really is no problem. Such arguments, however, have nothing to do with the measurement of national savings. They are arguments about why national savings are low. An economist who tells you that there is really less of a budget deficit problem than there seems to be is simply telling you that the causes of low national saving lie elsewhere than in the Federal budget. Maybe he's right—but it still remains true that the United States as a whole is saving very much less than it used to.

Figure 15 shows how national savings as a percentage of national income has changed over the past 20 years. Except during the recession years 1974–1975, the national savings rate in the 1970s remained roughly what it had been in the 1950s and 1960s—about 7 percent of income. Then during the 1980s the rate plunged to the astonishingly low level of 2 percent. Although the savings rate recovered somewhat in 1988 and 1989, it still remains far below its historical level.

The low level of U.S. national savings is particularly striking when we compare our experience with that of other countries. While the United States recently has been saving just 2 to 3 percent of its income, other industrial countries have been saving an average of 10 percent, and Japan has been saving no less than 18 percent.

What are the consequences of low national saving? Recall the definition: national saving is the sum of net domestic and net foreign investment. If savings fall, then domestic investment or foreign investment, or both, must give.

In America's case, the sharp fall in our savings was reflected in slightly lower domestic investment. The most dramatic effect, however, was the decline in our net foreign investment. In the 1970s the United States continued to invest slightly more abroad than foreigners invested here, so our position as a net creditor in the

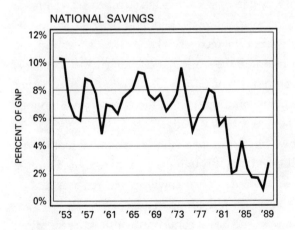

Figure 15
During the 1970s the United States continued to save about the same fraction of its national income as it had in the 1950s and 1960s. After 1980, however, national savings plunged to the lowest level seen in the postwar period.

world economy continued to grow. When national savings crashed in the 1980s, however, the United States maintained its rate of investment by becoming a massive net importer of capital—initially by selling foreigners large quantities of bonds, and increasingly by attracting foreigners eager to buy controlling interests in American businesses.

The main consequence of the decline in U.S. saving, then, has been a growing dependence on foreign capital to finance our investment—the flip side of the unprecedented trade deficits of the 1980s.

Why were savings so low in the 1980s? There are two main reasons. First, as everyone knows (but some people choose to deny), the huge Federal budget deficit meant that the Federal government was engaged in massive dis-saving (or negative saving); that accounts for about half of the decline in saving since the late 1970s. The other big factor was a sharp decline in saving by households; as families reduced their savings and loaded up on consumer credit, the personal savings rate fell to record lows.

Nobody is sure why personal savings fell so much, or whether it will bounce back. Some economists think that personal savings is showing signs of a partial recovery: There was a jump in the personal savings rate after the stock market crash in October 1987, reflecting a new caution on the part of consumers; this new higher rate has persisted. If it continues to rise, then the national savings problem will be somewhat alleviated.

Meanwhile, however, the national savings rate still remains very low by historical standards, bringing with it an inevitable huge trade deficit. Since the trade deficit is widely viewed as a serious problem, why don't we do something to raise savings?

The answer is simple and has become boring through repetition: The only *reliable* way to raise national savings is to eliminate the budget deficit. Although some economists claim that reducing the budget deficit would do little to increase national savings, the reasonable citizen's view is still that a lower budget deficit is the one surefire route to higher national savings. Special incentives, tax reform, and who knows what else might help, or they might not. Eliminating the budget deficit will.

Apologists for the budget deficit

To the extent that there is an orthodox position on the deficit, within both the Republican and Democratic parties, it is the one laid out in the previous section: The budget deficit reduces national saving, helping cause the trade deficit, and should therefore be eliminated. (Where the parties differ is in how.) The deficit, however, has its defenders, on both the left and the right. While the mainstream of both the economics profession and the political community condemns the deficit, self-proclaimed experts have, with vigor and not a little glee, taken on the role of apologists for, and even champions of, the deficit.

The harmless deficit: The view from the left

The defense of the deficit from the left has come from a number of academics and journalists, but the most influential has been Northwestern's Robert Eisner, a past president of the American Economic Association, and an economist with impeccable mainstream credentials. Eisner's argument, at bottom, is that the deficit is a statistical illusion. He rests his case on two points: the effects of inflation in raising the measured deficit, and the difference between the current and capital expenditures of the government.

The inflation point may best be explained by example. Imagine a government with a total debt of a trillion dollars, paying 4 percent

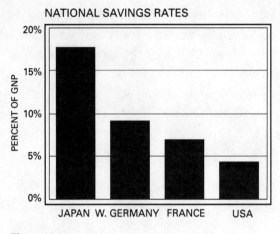

NATIONAL SAVINGS RATES

Figure 16
The United States saves far less of its national income than other major industrial
countries.

interest on the debt, so its total interest bill is $40 billion. Now im-
agine the same situation, but with an inflation rate of 5 percent—
and, because inflation tends to pull up the rate of interest, an
interest rate of 9 percent. Interest payments on the debt will then be
$90 billion, and the government deficit will be $50 billion larger
than in the first example.

But does the government really do the economy any more harm
in the second case than in the first? The government itself does not
consume any more goods and services. Nor does the larger deficit
encourage higher consumption: Owners of government bonds will
understand perfectly well that the higher interest rate they receive
is offset by the erosion in the value of the bonds by inflation, so they
will not feel richer. So the larger deficit in the second case won't lead
to higher consumption by either the public or the private sector. But
since national saving is simply income less consumption, that
means the higher measured deficit will not have a negative effect on
national saving.

Eisner calculates that as a result of this inflation illusion, the national deficit of $150 billion is overstated by about $80 billion.

Next he argues that a good chunk of the government's spending is investment, not consumption, building roads, aircraft carriers, and other long-lived assets. One should not count this as part of the government's current expenditure any more than a firm's investment spending is counted against its profits. Thus Eisner concludes that there really isn't any deficit if you measure it right, and we should all relax about the deficit issue. In fact, Eisner and others argue that the really damaging thing is not the deficit but the attack on the deficit, which distorts public priorities.

What's wrong with Eisner's argument? The main problem seems to be that he ignores the context. First, if his arguments are true now, they were even more true ten years ago. At the end of the 1970s inflation was much higher than it is now. Furthermore, the attempts to hold down government expenditure in the 1980s have, by most accounts, cut the amount of government *investment* much more than the amount of government *consumption*—if complaints about deteriorating infrastructure are taken seriously, we may even have negative *net* government investment. So a calculation along Eisner's lines leads to the conclusion that under Jimmy Carter the Federal government was running a huge surplus! Whether you agree with the measurement is less important than the fact that, however you measure it, the Federal government moved sharply *toward* deficit in the 1980s, and thus contributed to the decline in national savings.

And here's where the second criticism of Eisner's argument comes in. Maybe there really isn't any government deficit, but we certainly do have a huge trade deficit. We cannot do much to cut this deficit unless national savings can be raised—and cutting the Federal deficit is the only reliable tool we have to do this. So if you are worried about the trade deficit, what difference does it make if Eisner can show that by some measure we don't have a budget deficit?

The harmless deficit: The view from the right

While some on the left deny that there is really a deficit, an influential group of economists on the right argues that it doesn't matter what the deficit is. The leader of this group is Robert Barro of Harvard, whose professional standing is, if anything, even greater than Eisner's. Barro and his followers maintain that as long as the U.S. government is solvent—which it clearly is—the actual size of the deficit is irrelevant.

Barro's argument may be conveyed by the following example. Suppose that the Federal government were to announce that it was reducing everyone's taxes this year, that it would cover the revenue loss by selling one-year bonds, and that it would levy a special tax surcharge next year to pay off the bonds. What would be the effect on consumer spending?

Barro says that there would be no effect. Everyone would realize that their higher income this year will be offset by lower income next year, and that they would need to put aside the current tax rebate to pay the higher future taxes. So, according to Barro, just about all of the tax reduction would be saved. The Federal deficit would rise, but so would private saving, and national saving would be unaffected.

Generalizing from this example, Barro and his followers contend that changes in tax rates have no effect on national saving. If the government raises taxes now, the reduced government debt will mean lower taxes later, and people will therefore not cut their current consumption.

Does this mean that nothing the government does will affect private spending? No—but what matters is how much the government spends, not how much it collects in taxes. If the government introduces a new spending program, then individuals will realize that this increases the amount of taxes they have to pay—if not now, then later with interest. So they will cut their consumption immediately. The point is not that what the government does is unimportant, but rather that the decision whether to tax now or later, to run a deficit or raise taxes immediately, is basically irrelevant.

Although this view of the deficit is highly abstract, it has two key features that help raise an economic theory to prominence. First, it appeals to the professional instincts of many economists, who always prefer to push the assumption of rational economic behavior as far as possible. Second, it serves a political end: The Barro view, however honestly held by its academic proponents, can be appropriated by apologists for the deficit record of Republicans in the White House. As a result, Barro's views have come to be taken very seriously, both by his colleagues and by intellectually minded conservatives.

Unfortunately, there is nothing in U.S. experience since 1980 that lends empirical support to the Barro view. When the Reagan Administration cut taxes without cutting aggregate spending, private savings did not rise—they fell. Moreover, Barro's theory requires that ordinary households be extremely well informed and rational about the future tax implications of current government spending—to a degree that seems quite unlikely. What fraction of the American public knows anything of substance about the Federal budget? The notion that ordinary Americans can readily form reasonable estimates of the budget's implications for their tax rates over the rest of their lives strains credulity. In practice, one does not often hear Barro's views expressed directly in Washington's corridors of power. But they do play an important role in maintaining a climate of doubt about whether the budget deficit is really a serious problem.

Reducing the deficit

Despite the deficit's apologists, political orthodoxy still demands that Congress and the Administration make a show of doing something about it. What are the options?

In fiscal 1989 it is likely that the Federal government will have expenditures of about $1.1 trillion, with revenues of $980 billion, for an accounting deficit of $120 billion. This number is partly a fraud, thanks to the desperate accounting expedients used to postpone the Gramm-Rudman targets; the true deficit is more like $150 billion. So roughly speaking revenues are only about 85 percent of expenditures.

Democrats would like to close this gap chiefly by raising taxes but are unwilling to take the lead; George Bush's lips have pledged that no such thing will happen, and therefore Republicans claim to intend to eliminate the deficit mainly by cutting nondefense spending.

The idea that the deficit can be cured largely by cutting nondefense spending is, if it is meant to describe an immediate policy option, nonsense. Figure 17 shows the main reason why. In essence, the Federal government spends the vast bulk of its money on three things: defense, social insurance programs (primarily Social Security) that mostly benefit the middle class, and interest on the national debt. Everything else—AIDS research, education, drug enforcement, antipoverty programs, foreign aid, and the cost of actually running the government—accounts for only 19 percent.

Those who speak about the need to cut government spending usually do not have defense spending or Social Security in mind, nor are they advocating repudiation of the national debt. But even radical cuts in what's left wouldn't eliminate the deficit. In any case, radical cuts are all but impossible. Many of the programs in the

COMPOSITION OF FEDERAL EXPENDITURE, 1987

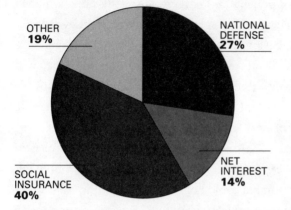

OTHER
19%

NATIONAL
DEFENSE
27%

NET
INTEREST
14%

SOCIAL
INSURANCE
40%

Figure 17
The bulk of Federal spending goes for defense, social insurance, and interest on
the Federal debt. This makes radical further cuts in total spending nearly
impossible.

"everything else" category have already been sharply curtailed
over the past eight years; meanwhile, demands for new spending,
for everything from the war on drugs to aid for Poland and the
savings and loan bailout, have been accumulating. So there is no
real possibility of closing the gap by cutting spending.[2]

---

2. The sudden collapse of Leninism has raised hopes that a "peace dividend"
may resolve America's budget woes. Such hopes are exaggerated, for a
variety of reasons. First, it is too soon to take events in Eastern Europe for
granted; surely there are more surprises in store, not all of them pleasant.
Second, Europe is not the world. While the end of the Cold War may allow a
reduction in U.S. forces in Germany, it will be a long time before the United
States can comfortably contemplate sharp cuts elsewhere. Third, advocates
of a strong defense argue that many cuts of recent years have been penny-
wise and pound-foolish; they will press to use the released resources within
the Pentagon. Lastly, the enthusiasm over the "peace dividend" already
suggests that the dividend will be spent, probably several times over, before
any real savings become available.

While the public may not know this, everyone in Washington does. What the opponents of tax increases really hope is not to *eliminate* the deficit by *cutting* spending, but to *reduce* it by *restraining* spending. The basic idea is that if the rate of growth of spending can be kept below the rate of growth of the economy, the deficit will gradually fade away without any need either to make sharp spending cuts or to raise tax rates.

The arithmetic of such an approach—dubbed a "flexible freeze" by Michael Boskin, Chairman of the President's Council of Economic Advisers—can seem very appealing. Imagine, for a moment, that the U.S. government could hold its total spending constant in real terms for the next five years, while the U.S. economy grew at 2.5 percent or more a year and tax revenues grew along with it. The budget deficit would then fall to less than a third of its current ratio to national income, and the ratio of Federal debt to GNP would begin to decline. For all intents and purposes the deficit problem would be solved, with no need for either spending cuts or new taxes.

In effect we have already seen the results of a flexible freeze in action. In fiscal 1985 the Federal budget deficit was $212 billion, or 5.3 percent of GNP. In fiscal 1988 it was $155 billion, or 3.2 percent of GNP. This deficit reduction was partly due to an increase in the Social Security tax. It was achieved in large part, however, by cutting the rate of growth of spending, scrapping plans for rapid increases in the Pentagon budget, and restraining virtually all other Federal programs. The hope of the Bush Administration is that this process can continue, and gradually whittle down the remaining deficit.

Unfortunately, that is unlikely to happen—unless the apparent unraveling of the Soviet empire allows genuinely sharp cuts in defense. The reason is that the United States will have a hard time getting away with zero real growth in spending, or anything close to it, in the years ahead. Partly, this is because the responsibilities of the government grow with the economy. As population, employment, and output grow, the country needs more air traffic controllers, more law enforcement, more policing of the environment, etc. So any attempt to avoid spending more means putting an increasing burden on programs that are already stretched to the breaking point. At the same time, efforts to keep the budget numbers artificially low during the Reagan years have left the Federal government with an abundance of past due bills.

So the truth is that it's going to be very hard to make rapid progress on reducing the deficit just by restraining spending. Yet for the time being, at least, tax increases are politically out of bounds. That means the budget deficit will remain a more or less permanent fixture on the American economic scene.

A day of reckoning?

If there were any justice in the world, there would be a dramatic end to the deficit story: The adverse consequences of the deficit would become spectacularly apparent in an economic crisis, and the public would rise up and throw the rascals out. But of course there isn't any justice in the world. While there are possibilities of disaster, they don't have to materialize. It is not only possible but probable that budget deficits at more or less the current level will continue for the rest of the century. There will be costs to these deficits, but they may never reach the crisis stage.

Why can America apparently be so irresponsible fiscally yet avoid drastic punishment? At least part of the answer is that even as short-term politics has come to rule the budget, apolitical professionals have placed themselves firmly back in control of monetary policy.

7   The Triumphant Fed

The Federal Reserve sits in the middle of official Washington, three minutes' walk from the State Department, ten minutes from the White House. Yet psychologically it is a world apart. There are no lobbyists crowding the halls, few television crews outside, no "photo opportunities." The senior officials are paid more than their counterparts in the Federal bureaucracy; there is no revolving door. Where the top four levels of the rest of the government are filled by short-term political appointees, the Federal Reserve consists of career technocrats top to bottom. It is a serious place, and a triumphant one. A decade ago the Federal Reserve was under attack, its independence threatened by a variety of ideological and political challenges. Those challenges were brilliantly met, and today the Fed remains as it was, the most powerful economic institution in the country.

What the Fed does

The Federal Reserve is what the British call a quango—a "quasi-nongovernmental organization." Its complex structure divides power between the Federal government and the private banks that are its members, and in effect gives substantial autonomy to a governing board of long-term appointees.

The Fed's power comes from its unique role in controlling the nation's supply of so-called "base money"—the sum total of the currency in the hands of the public and the reserves that banks are legally required to hold to back their deposits. Banks can withdraw their reserves in the form of cash, or deposit cash with the Fed to add to their reserves. But the total quantity of base money cannot be changed except by the Fed's action.

By injecting or withdrawing base money from the system, the Fed has immense influence over the economy. Suppose that the Fed puts more cash in—which it usually does by buying U.S. government debt from a select group of commercial banks. These banks then find themselves with more reserves than they are legally required to hold. They lend out the excess, expanding credit and driving down interest rates. Furthermore, most of the money they lend out ends up being deposited back in the banking system, allowing a second wave of lending, a third, and so on. The result is that the Fed's injection of base money has a multiplier effect, expanding credit throughout the economy. The rise in credit and the fall in interest rates, in turn, stimulates the economy through a variety of channels: housing starts rise, the dollar falls (stimulating exports), business investment rises, consumer credit gets easier. Conversely, if the Federal Reserve withdraws base money from the economy, the process runs in reverse: credit contracts, and the whole economy is restrained.

What is important about the Fed's power to control the economy is how swift and technical its actions can be. Other kinds of economic policy take time and often legislation: tax changes and public works programs take years to craft. The Federal Reserve, meanwhile, can pull the economy out of a recession or (if it makes a mistake) push it into an inflationary boom, cool down an overheated economy or (if it makes the opposite mistake) create a slump—all with nothing more than an instruction to the open market desk in New York to buy or sell.

How should the Fed use this power? The answer its staff has always preferred is "with discretion." That is, they prefer to be left alone, trusted to do the right thing without any specific targets or guidelines. That's the situation they are in now. But they almost lost it, and how the Fed kept its independence was one of the key economic stories of the 1980s.

Monetarists, gold bugs, and rational expectations

The Federal Reserve, like so much of the country, was scarred by the Vietnam War, but not in the usual way. The Fed's sin was that when faced with Lyndon Johnson's determination to have both guns and butter, it failed to do its job. Instead of tightening money to keep the economy from overheating, it tried to hold interest rates down. The result was a gradual acceleration of inflation during the second half of the 1960s, from near-stable prices to the 4 to 5 percent inflation that passes for stability today.

After a half-hearted attempt to bring down inflation during the first Nixon Administration, the Fed did something worse: It allowed a rapid expansion of the economy in 1972–1973, which brought on inflationary pressures from the demand side just as the collapse of an attempt at wage and price controls combined with soaring oil prices to give inflation a huge push from the other side. The result was the worst inflation America had seen since the Civil War. Worse yet, it was difficult to shake off the suspicion that Federal Reserve Board Chairman Arthur Burns took risks with inflation to ensure the reelection of Richard Nixon—a suspicion without any solid evidence to back it, but one that nevertheless haunts the long memories of the Fed.

When inflation took off yet again, in 1979, the Federal Reserve's credibility was badly shaken. The Fed was soon faced with a variety of proposals to strip it of much of its autonomy. What made this effort particularly dangerous, from the Fed's point of view, was the fact that the opponents of an independent Fed had acquired a considerable intellectual cachet.

Since the 1950s, so-called monetarists, led by the University of Chicago's Milton Friedman, have persistently argued that the Federal Reserve, instead of making monetary policy, should follow a simple monetary rule. The essence of the monetarist argument is that discretionary policy on the part of the Fed actually makes the economy less stable, like a driver alternately stomping on the brakes and flooring the gas pedal. Friedman wanted the economy to be put on cruise control. Based on historical studies of the relationship between money and income, Friedman argued that if the Federal Reserve would simply ensure that the money supply grew at a steady rate, say, 4 percent a year, the economy would also grow steadily and without inflation. Between the 1950s and the end of the 1970s, Friedman's arguments gradually took root in educated opinion, changing from scorned iconoclasm to orthodoxy.

After Friedman came the gold bugs, a collection of conservative journalists and politicians whose intellectual clout was supplied by Columbia University's brilliant, eccentric Robert Mundell. The gold bugs argued that even Friedman's rigid targets for the Federal Reserve were not strong enough. A truly sound monetary policy would only come by tying money to an objective outside standard, such as gold.[3] In the 1930s John Maynard Keynes dismissed the monetary role of gold as a "barbarous relic"; yet by the 1980s the call for a return to gold had achieved widespread respectability, capped by a series of gala conferences jointly hosted by Senator Bill Bradley (D-NJ) and Representative Jack Kemp (R-NY).

---

3. A gold standard would be much more extreme than Friedman's rule because it would amount to fixing the quantity of base money. Friedman wanted the Fed to target "monetary aggregates" that included deposits as well as base money; he was aware that even with constant base money large changes in these aggregates could destabilize the economy. For example, at the onset of the Depression the supply of base money in the United States remained constant, but thanks to a banking crisis Friedman's monetary aggregates declined by a third.

Either a full adoption of monetarism or, worse, a revival of the gold standard would take away much of the independence of the Federal Reserve and shift its function from the making of economic policy to narrow technical issues. And that, of course, was the point. Both the monetarists and the gold bugs drew much of their intellectual justification from the influential doctrine of rational expectations. Loosely speaking, this doctrine holds not only that inflation feeds on itself via expectations of future inflation (a common view among economists), but that inflation could be cured quickly and with little pain if the commitment of the monetary authorities not to accommodate inflation could be made credible to the public. Tie the Fed's hands, said the enthusiasts—with rigid monetary targets, or better yet with a gold standard—and we will almost immediately have stable prices with hardly any recession.

The staffers at the Federal Reserve have never been monetarists, and certainly not advocates of a gold standard. They have always believed that their sophisticated judgment would outperform any mechanical rule. In 1979, however, with double-digit inflation, they found it hard to persuade the rest of the country of their competence. The ultimate success of the Fed in persuading the nation that it really does know best was a spectacular example of "judo politics": using the strength of one's opponents to win.

Volcker's victory

In October 1979 the Federal Reserve, under the leadership of Paul Volcker, made a dramatic announcement: Henceforth it would make the targeting of monetary aggregates its chief priority. Publicly, it appeared that monetarism had prevailed.

Three years later the Fed announced that it was abandoning its monetary targets for the year. Since then it has repeatedly done the same, and the targets have attracted steadily less attention. So the

Fed, if it was ever monetarist, was monetarist for less than three years.

In retrospect, it seems clear what happened. The Federal Reserve was never monetarist. But it did need to win a major victory against inflation—both for the sake of the economy and to preserve its own treasured independence. It also knew that victory over inflation wouldn't come cheap (rational expectations had few friends at the Fed). The only reliable victory, in its view, would require a deep recession. The question was: How could the Fed persuade the country to swallow such bitter medicine?

Monetarism was the perfect answer. The Fed never said: "We propose to put the country through the worst recession since the 1930s, so that unemployment and excess capacity force the inflation rate down." It simply gave in to its critics and adopted monetary targets. Trying to meet these targets, not incidentally, meant putting the economy through the wringer. But who could criticize the Fed when all it was doing was what its most vociferous critics had been urging all along?

By the late summer of 1982 U.S. inflation was subsiding, but the recession seemed in danger of spiraling out of control. The sudden emergence of the Third World debt crisis raised fears of financial chaos. The result? The Fed cast off its monetarist cloak and returned to an active, discretionary policy. The money spigots were opened, and the economy began a rapid economic recovery. Subsequently the Fed has felt free to fine-tune—reining in the money supply when it fears a resurgence of inflation, pumping it up when the recovery seems to be flagging. In other words, the Fed went back to its traditional position that it knows best, and should not be tied down by someone else's rules.

For those concerned with the long-term independence of the Federal Reserve, the results could not have been better. The limited victory over inflation restored the country's confidence in monetary policy. The pain of the recession was quickly forgotten as the economy recovered. And despite occasional sniping from the White House, the Reagan-Bush Administration had little to complain about: The pain came early in Reagan's first term, the recovery came soon enough to fuel a landslide in 1984, and it continued long enough to let Bush coast in four years later.

From a monetarist perspective, Federal Reserve policy since 1982 has been nothing short of scandalous. The rate of money growth has shifted erratically, sometimes rising to double digits, sometimes becoming negative. For several years after the abandonment of targets, monetarists—Friedman in particular—routinely forecast a disastrous acceleration of inflation and/or a severe recession as a result of monetary instability. Yet the actual result has been remarkably smooth sailing, with both the inflation rate and the rate of GNP growth far more stable in the second half of the 1980s than they had been for a long time.

There are still monetarists, but they almost seem like relics now. Milton Friedman's forecasts of doom were at first taken seriously, then ridiculed, then ignored. The gold standard still has friends at the *Wall Street Journal*, but in few other places. At least for now the Fed is where it wants to be: independent, trusted, and not too closely scrutinized.

Risks to the Fed

The Federal Reserve is currently in a strong position, based upon its perceived success. Yet there is in that position a basic vulnerability of which the Fed is all too well aware.

The problem is that the United States has two major economic worries—the trade deficit *and* inflation—while the Federal Reserve has just one policy instrument: control over money and credit. The textbooks tell us that monetary policy needs to be supplemented

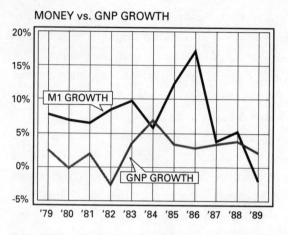

Figure 18
Monetary growth has been very erratic since the Federal Reserve abandoned its monetarist approach in 1982. Yet output and inflation have been remarkably stable.

with fiscal policy to achieve macroeconomic goals. Translated, that means that you can't count on having both acceptable inflation and acceptable trade performance unless you are willing to do something about your budget deficit as well as your money supply. With the Federal deficit trapped in political amber, however, the Federal Reserve bears the entire burden of stabilizing the economy.

So far, the Fed has been both lucky and skillful in reconciling these goals. It has kept inflation under control, and the trade deficit has remained tolerable. But there is a lurking danger that growing pressures to do something about the trade deficit will undermine the commitment to keeping inflation down. There is continuing political pressure on the Federal Reserve to adopt "soft money" policies that would keep interest rates and the dollar low, even at the risk of inflation. Should the Fed give in to these pressures, the end result could easily be an inflationary resurgence—squandering the gains won at such enormous cost.

This is not academic speculation. The recent experience of Britain shows that a seemingly stable monetary situation can unravel with sickening speed. In 1987 the position of the Bank of England, the Fed's counterpart, seemed as strong as that of the Fed. Inflation, which in Britain had exceeded 20 percent in the 1970s, was down to less than 4 percent. Britain's trade position was acceptable—indeed, the U.K. actually ran a small current account surplus in 1986. Then everything fell apart. A runaway domestic boom drove the unemployment rate down from 10 to 6.5 percent. The Bank of England, fearing that a tight monetary policy would create an overvalued pound, failed to rein in demand, thereby aggravating a rapidly widening trade deficit. In the end the British managed to get the worst of both worlds. Inflation accelerated to more than 8 percent, and the current account deficit surged to more than 4 percent of GNP (far worse than America's). Interest rates went from 8 to 13 percent, the Chancellor of the Exchequer quit, and the Thatcher government found itself in crisis.

Could the Federal Reserve find itself in the same situation? Absolutely. Mainstream estimates suggest that the U.S. current account deficit will deteriorate markedly in 1990 and 1991. Unless U.S. domestic demand providentially slackens, the Federal Reserve will be presented with an agonizing choice: It will either have to try to bring down the dollar to contain the trade problem, and risk an inflationary surge on the British model, or focus on inflation and face both direct pressure and the risk of a protectionist reaction in the United States.

So the triumph of the Fed may represent only a brief moment in the sun. To understand the risks, however, we need to spend some more time on the interlinked issues of the dollar and protectionism.

8   The Dollar

The gyrations of U.S. dollar policy must often seem mysterious to even the most intelligent laymen. First we liked our dollar strong: In early 1985 Ronald Reagan, in a widely quoted speech, pointed to the strength of the dollar on foreign exchange markets as proof of the success of U.S. economic policies. But soon afterward we wanted it weak: In September 1985 Treasury Secretary James Baker, in a widely praised move, convened a meeting at the Plaza Hotel in New York at which the major industrial countries agreed to try to drive the dollar down. Then we changed our minds again: The same countries agreed in another meeting, at the Louvre in February 1987, to stabilize exchange rates—which initially meant holding the dollar up.

Apparently, this effort was too successful: Through much of 1989 the Japanese and the Europeans tried without much success to keep the dollar from rising.

Through all these policy zigs and zags the economic experts have offered a running commentary that is even more confusing than usual, with some economists insisting that the dollar is grossly undervalued even as others argue that it is greatly overvalued. What's all this about?

To make sense of the dollar issue, it is necessary to ask what purpose dollar policy is supposed to serve. The answer is that we are trying to use dollar policy to help reduce our trade deficit. The reason there is so much confusion is that there are three unsettled points. First, are we really serious about reducing our trade deficit? Second, if we are, does trying to manage the dollar help? And third, if a managed dollar helps, where should it go?

Are we serious about reducing the trade deficit?

Arguably the United States has no real interest in getting its trade deficit down. As previously noted, our trade deficit does not really cost us jobs; the only certain harm it does is to increase our foreign debt, saddling future generations with the burden of paying our current bills. However, unless we are prepared to raise domestic saving, which basically means a sizable cut in the budget deficit, any attempt to reduce the trade deficit will come at the expense of higher interest rates and lower investment. There is a good case to be made that the United States should worry about savings, but not about the trade deficit.

Now we cannot run trade deficits forever. But, as Herbert Stein has pointed out, the nice thing about things that cannot go on forever is that they won't. Why not, then, simply rely on the market? A trade deficit poses no problem so long as foreign investors are willing to finance it, and it will correct itself as soon as they are not. So why have an active government policy of reducing the trade gap?

There are three standard arguments for such a policy, two economic and one political.

First, while trade deficits do always correct themselves, history suggests that the process is not always gentle. To take the most worrisome example, through the 1970s and the early 1980s Latin America ran persistent large deficits, which foreign investors seemed happy to finance. As late as 1981 the general consensus was that

Latin America could continue to borrow extensively for years to come. Yet in less than a year there was a collapse of financing that forced Latin American economies to cut imports by as much as two-thirds, plunging the region into a deep slump from which it still has not emerged. With the benefit of hindsight, it is clear that the governments of Latin America should have worried about their trade deficits, and taken steps to bring them down, while foreign financing was still easy, instead of waiting for the crunch.

The second argument, related to the first, is that reducing the trade deficit takes time. Firms do not change suppliers, or consumers shift to different products, overnight. Turning a trade deficit around often means building new capacity, new distribution networks, and so on. The U.S. experience with the declining dollar is illustrative. The dollar began declining in early 1985, yet the trade deficit actually continued to rise until mid-1987. If we think that the trade deficit will or should begin to shrink sometime in the future, even if the event is two or three years off, it is a good idea to start giving firms incentives to increase exports and reduce imports now. Of course, if the market could be counted on to be farsighted, if exchange rates and the investment plans of firms could be counted on to reflect a careful appreciation of long-term prospects, no special policy would be needed here. But nothing in recent experience suggests that markets are particularly farsighted.

Third, dollar politics cannot be separated from trade politics. The trade deficit feeds protectionist pressures in the United States. Unless that deficit can be seen to be declining, it may be impossible for an Administration, no matter how free trade–minded, to contain those pressures.

So there is a case for having a policy of getting the trade deficit down. It is not a watertight case—reasonable people can and do argue that the trade deficit should not be a public policy concern—

but as a practical matter the U.S. government does worry about the trade deficit and hopes to see it decline.

Hopes are not, of course, the same as actions. The orthodox recipe for reducing a trade deficit is to combine currency depreciation with fiscal austerity. The United States has been willing to try the first, but not the second. So we can legitimately ask whether it makes sense to try to do anything about the dollar until there are clear signs that a budget solution is in sight.

The answer is a definite maybe. National savings may be on the rise—even without dramatic action on the budget. That makes room for some reduction in the trade deficit.

Furthermore, there is another piece that should be brought into the picture: Most estimates suggest that at the current level of the dollar the U.S. trade position will actually *worsen* substantially over the next few years. So we may need to do something just to keep the trade deficit from rising.[4]

Lastly, given the political dangers arising from protectionism, it makes some sense to take risks in order to keep the trade deficit down. The efforts to bring down the dollar after 1985 were con-

---

4. There are four reasons to expect the U.S. current account deficit to rise substantially from this point. First, the dollar is now substantially above its levels in 1987 and 1988. Since the exchange rate affects trade flows with a long lag, the trade numbers of 1989 really reflect the exchange rate of two years previously; when the higher current dollar gets reflected in trade, the trade deficit will get larger. Second, as U.S. foreign debt grows, interest payments, dividends, and other investment income paid to foreigners will increase. Third, even if U.S. exports and imports grow at the same rate, the deficit will grow because exports are so much smaller than imports. Lastly, declining competitiveness means that the U.S. trade deficit tends to widen unless the dollar falls steadily over time. Thus, most trade forecasters expect to see substantial increases in the current account deficit unless the dollar falls. William Cline of the Institute for International Economics forecasts a deficit that widens from the 1988 number of $125 billion to $200 billion by 1992; his numbers are similar to those forecast by the IMF and the Federal Reserve.

demned by all the predictable voices as dangerously inflationary; in retrospect things turned out just fine.[5]

Yet, as noted in the last chapter, there are serious risks in putting too much emphasis on trade deficit reduction. In fact, the case for getting the trade deficit down is much weaker than the case for using a lower dollar to get there.

Dollar policy

The principal tool that the United States has to influence its trade balance is the value of the dollar on foreign exchange markets. The conventional wisdom holds that if the dollar's price in terms of foreign currencies can be reduced, U.S. goods will become more competitive on world markets, and the trade deficit will fall. That is why we had a deliberate policy of reducing the value of the dollar in 1985 and 1986, why the major economies have been trying to hold the dollar down in 1989, and why many economists and policymakers (most notably the staff of the International Monetary Fund) argue that the dollar needs to fall still lower.

As in so many areas of economics, this conventional wisdom is under attack from both right and left. On both sides, it is alleged that reducing the foreign exchange value of the dollar is ineffective at reducing the trade deficit, and harmful in other ways. These attacks have been fed by the fact that the results of dollar depreciation have been disappointing so far—of which more in a minute. But first let's look at what the critics say.

---

5. As always, there are voices on the other side. The same Robert Eisner who argues that there really isn't any Federal budget deficit is harshly critical of the Fed for "guarding excessively against inflation" and keeping the dollar strong. Eisner would have an all-out push to drive the dollar down.

The attack from the right has, as usual, more powerful support—notably the *Wall Street Journal*. Conservative advocates of a gold standard, which would preclude any devaluation of the dollar, are naturally opposed to the idea that changing exchange rates can do any good. They therefore are attracted to the arguments of such people as Stanford's Ronald McKinnon, Columbia's Robert Mundell, and supply-side enthusiast Jude Wanniski, who claim that:

(1) the trade deficit is determined by the balance between savings and investment, not the value of the dollar, so depreciating the dollar can't help reduce it;

(2) depreciating the dollar leads to U.S. inflation, which will wipe out any apparent gains in the cost competitiveness of American industry.

Like most appealing but wrong arguments, this one starts from some valid observations. The trade deficit *does* ultimately depend on the balance between savings and investment, and depreciating the dollar *can* lead to inflation that wipes out competitive gains. But since the exchange rate plays such a crucial role in translating

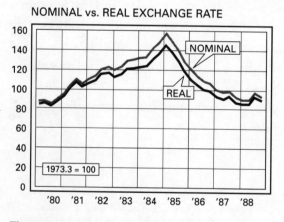

NOMINAL vs. REAL EXCHANGE RATE

Figure 19
The decline of the dollar was reflected almost one-for-one in a reduction of the prices of U.S. goods and services relative to those of foreigners.

changes in national savings or investment demand into changes in the trade deficit, it is odd to suppose that changing the price of U.S. goods relative to foreign by 25 or 50 percent somehow doesn't affect what we buy and sell.

As for the argument that dollar depreciation just produces inflation, not a real improvement in competitiveness, this merely shows the perennial popularity of ideology over evidence. From 1985 to 1987, the dollar fell almost 50 percent against the West German mark and the Japanese yen. Did U.S. prices double? Was there even a sharp acceleration in U.S. inflation? No. In fact, the dollar's fall was reflected almost exactly one-for-one in a change in the *real* exchange rate—the price of U.S. goods and services relative to those in other countries.

The attack from the left focuses on a different issue: foreign trade policy. Critics of dollar depreciation such as journalist Robert Kuttner argue that it is pointless to try to reduce the trade deficit by reducing the value of the dollar. Why? Because our foreign competitors simply won't allow American goods in.

Again, the evidence on the whole contradicts this view. If the basic problem is that foreign markets are closed to the United States, here's what we would expect to see when the dollar falls: U.S. imports would fall because U.S. consumers would switch to cheaper domestic products; but U.S. exports would not rise because foreigners would not admit our goods. In fact, what happened when the dollar fell was just the opposite. U.S. exports grew very rapidly, but the trade balance didn't improve much because U.S. imports also kept growing. This suggests that the problem is not so much America's lack of access to foreign markets as its taste for foreign imports. (There is a caveat to all of this. We do have a problem exporting to one country: Japan. For the problem of reducing the U.S. trade deficit, this is only a partial obstacle, since Japan is only part of the world. But for American trade policy, Japan is the central problem, as we shall see.)

Can driving the dollar down help reduce the trade deficit? On this issue the conventional wisdom wins, hands down: Yes, it can.

How far is down?

The decline of the dollar from 1985 to 1987 had an unmistakable impact on the U.S. trade position. From 1981 to 1986, the volume of U.S. imports rose inexorably, while U.S. exports stagnated; since 1986, exports have grown much more rapidly than imports. But the result has been disappointing to policymakers here and abroad. After all, in 1980 the United States actually exported more goods and services than it imported. By 1987 just about all of the dollar's rise had been reversed. Against some currencies, notably the yen, the dollar was weaker than it had ever been. Yet the U.S. foreign deficit remains well into triple digits. In 1989 the United States was expected to run a current account deficit of about $130 billion. Most forecasters expect that the deficit will be larger in 1990, and respon-

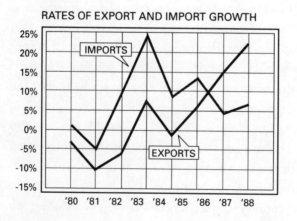

RATES OF EXPORT AND IMPORT GROWTH

Figure 20
The falling dollar sparked a U.S. export boom, but imports kept on rising, so the trade deficit did not fall as much as hoped.

sible estimates suggest that by 1992 the number could rise to $200 billion.

There are two obvious, related questions here: Why didn't the fall in the dollar do more? And how far does the dollar have to fall?

Let's put the first question a little more pointedly. Since late 1986 the dollar generally has been lower against most foreign currencies than it was in 1980. Yet at the beginning of the 1980s the United States exported more manufactured goods than it imported. In 1988 and 1989 our imports of manufactures consistently exceeded our exports by $100 billion or more each year. Why didn't the lower dollar do more?

The most important answer is probably the obvious one: The United States is just not as competitive as it used to be. Once upon a time we could sell our goods on world markets, even with a very strong dollar, because of our technical superiority. America made things nobody else could, and it produced goods known for their quality. Today the United States often lags behind Japan and even Western Europe in technology, and at least in consumer goods we have developed an impressive reputation for shoddiness. So even though the dollar is back where it used to be, the United States is not able to sell as much on world markets as it was.

This is not a new development. The 1980 dollar was much weaker than the 1970 dollar, yet the U.S. trade position in 1980 was about the same as it was in 1970. In other words, although the United States was fairly successful at selling its goods on world markets throughout the 1970s, it was able to do so only because of a dollar that weakened steadily against foreign currencies. Apparently this trend continued through the 1980s. The falling dollar has been chasing a moving target.

Figure 21 shows a suggestive picture that may help explain the persistence of the U.S. trade deficit. It shows the actual course of the dollar since 1970, as well as a trend line that tracks the change in the

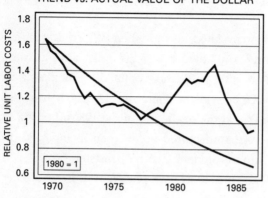

Figure 21
The dollar apparently needs to fall steadily over time if the United States is to balance its trade.

dollar from 1970 to 1980 and then continues downward at the same rate through the 1980s. What the picture reveals is that, despite the decline in the dollar since 1985, the dollar has been much stronger relative to its long-run downward trend in the 1980s than it was in the 1970s. So in a way we should not be surprised to find that the decline in the dollar has not done more to reduce the trade deficit.

But how far is down? Figure 21 suggests that the dollar would have to fall about 25 percent from its current level to be back on the trend line. Estimates from William Cline of the Institute for International Economics broadly agree: He finds that to reduce the U.S. current account deficit to $50 billion by 1992, the dollar would have to fall about 20 percent from its current level, and much more against the yen and the mark. (His estimates imply an exchange rate of less than 100 yen to the dollar, versus a rate in early 1990 of more than 140.) Cline and others who make similar estimates aren't necessarily right, but they are being both honest and careful, and their record in forecasting trade is pretty good. So the answer to the question "How far is down?" is "A long way."

Should the dollar be driven down?

To eliminate the U.S. trade deficit, or even to reduce it to modest proportions, probably requires driving the dollar down substantially from its current level. Yet the recent trend has actually been one of a rising dollar, opposed but not prevented by official action. Why don't we make dollar depreciation a priority?

One good reason has already been pointed out. We aren't actually serious about getting the trade deficit down—at least not yet. The textbook recipe for curing a trade deficit calls for a lower dollar combined with a lower budget deficit. If we have no intention of actually cutting the deficit any time soon, then it's too soon to seek a lower dollar.

Other, less good reasons have also been mentioned: right-wing claims that a lower dollar would be both ineffective and inflationary, and left-wing charges that dollar depreciation is pointless in the face of foreign barriers to American products at any price.

There is one additional argument—associated with trade policy hard-liners like Clyde Prestowitz and Robert Kuttner—which we are likely to hear more of in the next few years. It goes like this: Depreciating the dollar is a bad way to reduce the trade deficit because it amounts to meeting international competition by cutting American wages, thus lowering the living standards of American workers. Kuttner, in particular, has derided economists who want to "devalue the dollar to the point where we are a poor country."

But if a lower dollar imposes too great a cost on living standards, what is the alternative? The answer of Kuttner, Prestowitz, and others is to rely on trade policy. Instead of lowering the dollar, they say, the United States should get tough and demand that foreign nations open their markets to U.S. goods. That way, the trade deficit can come down without the need to cut U.S. wages.

This is an appealing argument, and not without some merit. It is also quite misleading, in two ways. First, it makes dollar depreciation sound much worse than it is. When the dollar falls by, say, 30 percent against the yen and the mark, a 30 percent reduction does occur in U.S. wages relative to those in Germany and Japan. But this is not the same as saying that U.S. real wages fall by 30 percent: They probably fall by no more than 1.5 percent. Why? Because even now most of the goods and services we consume are made at home, and a fairly large part of our imports tend to be priced in dollars, too. Second, the idea that the United States can realistically expect to get trade concessions from other countries that would be an adequate substitute for a lower dollar is wishful thinking.

Yet the trade deficit, and the frustrations of dollar policy, inevitably put the alternative of protectionism on the table. And if the trade deficit grows, as seems likely, then protectionism is sure to become more and more appealing to many politicians.

9   Free Trade & Protectionism

When future historians list the achievements of the United States during the 45 or so years that it acted as the undisputed leader of the world's democracies, special emphasis is sure to be given to the creation of a relatively free and open world trading system. From about 1950 until the early 1970s, protectionist barriers to world trade came down steadily, and world trade grew rapidly. Nearly everyone thinks that this growth in trade was a good thing.

Yet there are now powerful forces in the United States working against free trade. Much of the argument for protectionism represents sheer interest-group politics: It comes from well-organized groups that are losing out to foreign competition and want protection, never mind the national interest. Yet not all the opponents of free trade are hired guns (and not all its supporters are disinterested, either). It's important to look at both the political sources of protectionism and its intellectual foundations.

The politics of protectionism

The basic rule of trade politics is that producers count more than consumers. The benefits of a trade restriction are usually concentrated on a relatively small, well-organized, and well-informed group of producers, while its costs are usually spread thinly over a large diffuse group of consumers. As a result, the beneficiaries of a trade restriction are usually much more effective politically than its victims.

The classic case in the United States is the import quota on sugar, which benefits a handful of domestic producers at a typical annual cost to consumers of $1 billion a year. This quota goes unchallenged, because the $5 average annual cost per person is so small that probably not one voter in 200 even knows that the import restriction exists.

But if consumers offer no effective opposition to protection, why is U.S. trade relatively free? Because *exporters* advocate free trade. Exporters by definition want access to foreign markets and are as well organized as import-competing producers. For the past 40 years the United States and other advanced countries have used this fact to provide a framework for maintaining relatively free trade. Trade policies are not set unilaterally; they are negotiated between countries.[6] In these negotiations, U.S. import restrictions must be traded off against the import restrictions of other countries, so that U.S. exporters become a powerful voice urging us to accept imports from other countries if they will accept our exports in return.

The source of new protectionist pressure is now obvious. When the United States is running a huge trade deficit, the exporters who want open markets are outnumbered by the import-competing groups who want protection. If in 1980 you had told trade specialists that America would run trade deficits of more than $100 billion for seven years on end, they would surely have predicted more, not less, protection than we have seen.

---

6. The framework for these negotiations is usually the celebrated General Agreement on Tariffs and Trade, or GATT. GATT negotiations take place in a series of "rounds," of which the current, due to be concluded in late 1990, is the so-called Uruguay Round. The Uruguay Round is widely regarded as a failure, in that it has not made much forward progress at a time when the international trading system desperately needs a boost.

The relatively mild protectionist reaction so far is a tribute to the strength of free-trade ideology in the United States. The question is how long this can last. It may be useful to think of the United States as having a "protectionist overhang": a backlog of potential protectionist reaction barely held in check. Fear of this reaction is one of the main reasons for worrying about the trade deficit. If the trade deficit continues, sooner or later the persistent demands for more protection are likely to become irresistible.

But what would be wrong with that? Is protectionism really a fate to be greatly feared?

The (limited) evils of protectionism

Although most policymakers in Washington are convinced that protectionism is a bad thing, few of them have any clear idea why. In popular arguments against protectionism, the usual warning is that protectionism threatens our jobs—the Smoot-Hawley tariff of 1931, we are told, caused the Depression, and history can repeat itself.

Although protectionism *is* usually a bad thing, it is worth pointing out that it isn't as bad as all that. Protectionism does not cost our economy jobs, any more than the trade deficit does: U.S. employment is essentially determined by supply, not demand. The claim that protectionism caused the Depression is nonsense; the claim that future protectionism will lead to a repeat performance is equally nonsensical.

The real harm done by protectionism is much more modest and mundane: It reduces the efficiency of the world economy. To the extent that countries limit each other's exports, they block the mutually beneficial process by which nations specialize in producing goods for which their knowledge and resources are particularly well fitted. They also fragment markets, preventing firms and industries from realizing economies of scale. A protectionist country is usually less productive and thus poorer than it would have been under free trade; a protectionist world economy almost always so. (See the accompanying box.)

Just how expensive is protectionism? The answer is a little embarrassing, because standard estimates of the costs of protection are actually very low. America is a case in point. While much U.S. trade takes place with few obstacles, we have several major protectionist measures, restricting imports of autos, steel, and textiles in particular. The combined costs of these major restrictions to the U.S. economy, however, are usually estimated at less than three-quarters of 1 percent of U.S. national income. Most of this loss, furthermore, comes from the fact that the import restrictions, in effect, form foreign producers into cartels that charge higher prices to U.S. consumers. So most of the U.S. losses are matched by higher foreign profits. From the point of view of the world as a whole, the negative effects of U.S. import restrictions on efficiency are therefore much smaller—around one-quarter of 1 percent of U.S. GNP.

Other countries are more protectionist than the United States, and in some Third World nations wildly inefficient protectionist policies have caused major economic losses. Among advanced countries, however, protectionism at current levels is not a first-class issue. Without a doubt the major industrial nations suffer more, in economic terms, from unglamorous problems like avoidable traffic congestion and unnecessary waste in defense contracting than they do from protectionism. To take the most extreme example, the cost to taxpayers of the savings and loan bailout alone will be at least five times as large as the annual cost to U.S. consumers of all U.S. import restrictions.

If the costs of protectionism are so mild, why does the defense of free trade loom so large on the public agenda? Symbolism and

THE COSTS OF TRADE CONFLICT

A hypothetical scenario may be useful for understanding what the costs of protection are, and why they are more modest than many people seem to think.

Let's imagine that most of the world's market economies were to group themselves into three trading blocs — one centered on the United States, one centered on the European Economic Community, and one centered on Japan. And let's suppose that each of these trading blocs becomes highly protectionist, imposing a tariff against goods from outside the bloc of 100 percent, which we suppose leads to a fall in imports of 50 percent.

So we are imagining a trade war that cuts the volume of world trade in half. What would be the costs of this trade war?

One immediate response would be that each bloc would lose jobs in the industries that formerly exported to the others. This is true; but each bloc would correspondingly gain a roughly equal number of jobs producing goods it formerly imported. There is no reason to expect that even such a major fragmentation of the world market would cause extra unemployment.

The cost would come instead from reduced efficiency. Each bloc would produce goods for itself that it could have imported more cheaply. With a 100 percent tariff, some goods would be produced domestically even though they could have been imported at half the price. For these goods there is thus a waste of resources equal to the value of the original imports.

But this would be true only of goods that would have been imported in the absence of tariffs, and even then 100 percent represents a maximum estimate. Our three hypothetical trading blocs would, however, import only about 10 percent of the goods and services they use from abroad even under free trade.

A trade war that cut international trade in half, and which caused an *average* cost of wasted resources for the displaced production of, say, 50 percent, would therefore cost the world economy only 2.5 percent of its income (50 percent × 5 percent = 2.5 percent).

This is not a trivial sum—but it is a long way from a Depression. (It is roughly the cost of a 1 percent increase in the unemployment rate.) And it is the result of an extreme scenario, in which protectionism has a devastating effect on world trade.

If the trade conflict were milder, the costs would be much less. Suppose that the tariff rates were only 50 percent, leading to a 30 percent fall in world trade. Then 3 percent of the goods originally used would be replaced with domestic substitutes, costing at most 50 percent more. If the typical domestic substitute costs 25 percent more, then the cost of the trade conflict is 0.75 percent of world income (25 percent × 3 percent = 0.75 percent).

politics. Ideologically, free trade is an important touchstone for advocates of free-market economics. As Paul Samuelson once pointed out, comparative advantage is one of the few ideas in economics that is true without being obvious. Politically, free trade is important as a counterweight to crude economic nationalism. So free trade has passionate defenders in a way that other, equally worthy causes—such as economically efficient environmental regulation—do not.

Even if protectionism isn't the most terrible thing in the world, however, it is still a bad thing. Or is it? While the great weight of educated opinion still condemns protection, there are some arguments in its favor.

Protection and the trade deficit

Arguments in favor of protection come in two basic forms. One argument wants the United States to use the *threat* of protection to extract concessions from foreign countries; those who use this argument are not advocating protection per se, but they are willing to use protection as a bargaining threat—a bluff that they are presumably willing to see carried out, at least occasionally. The other argument takes protection to be an intrinsically good thing, at least in some cases.

The bargaining argument for protection is usually stated in the context of the problem of lowering the trade deficit. The United States needs to reduce its trade deficit, say the advocates of this position; but driving down the dollar is ineffective because of foreign trade barriers and reduces American living standards. So let's instead expand our exports by threatening to limit our imports: This will force foreigners to open their markets and allow us to reduce the trade deficit without the need for a much lower dollar.

The main problem with this proposal is that it won't work. It is just not realistic to expect increased access to foreign markets to make more than a minor contribution to reducing the U.S. trade deficit, with or without U.S. pressure. The reasons are both economic and political.

First, the economics. When we talk about removing foreign barriers to U.S. exports, what do we mean? Despite the rhetoric, there are only a few major legislated foreign programs that have a large identifiable impact on U.S. exports; most of these are in the agricultural area. If Japan opened its rice market, or Europe canceled its agricultural support programs, this would help U.S. exports, but it would fall far short of curing our trade deficit. [7]

Meanwhile, there are political realities. U.S. pressure is simply not going to force radical changes in economic policy abroad. The major barriers to American exports are programs, like Europe's agricultural policy, with powerful domestic constituencies. American pressure may induce marginal changes in these programs, but it is a fantasy to imagine that by getting tough we can force other countries to abandon them. The U.S. economy is no bigger than Europe's, and not much bigger than Japan's. Politicians in other countries answer primarily to domestic interests, just as ours do. We cannot expect to bully Europe or Japan into doing things our way any more than they could expect to do the same to us.

Given these economic and political realities, the proposal to use the threat of protection to solve the trade deficit will, in practice, inevitably degenerate into the implementation of that threat. To say

---

7. There is a special issue of access to the Japanese market, which is less of a matter of identifiable restrictions than of the whole structure of Japan's economy; we'll come back to that in the next chapter. But even if something could be done to remove the "structural impediments" to imports in Japan, it would not make a large difference to U.S. exports.

that you favor using potential import quotas as a way to spur U.S. exports is, in the end, disingenuous: The result will almost always be fewer imports rather than more exports.

Indeed, however much they may talk about spurring exports, the advocates of a tougher trade policy seem much more interested in limiting imports. Robert Kuttner's own manifesto on trade policy, which advocates a broad system of "managed trade," takes as its model the Multi-Fiber Arrangement: an international treaty that purely and simply restricts trade in textiles and apparel. That is, in the end he views protectionism not as a bargaining chip but as a permanent policy.

But what's so bad about that? We have just seen that the conventionally measured costs of protection are not very large. And there are intellectually respectable arguments suggesting that protection may, in some cases, actually be beneficial.

The economic case for protection

Economic theories matter, though not necessarily in the ways that their creators might have wished. In the 1970s public finance economists, Martin Feldstein prominent among them, worked hard to persuade the economics profession that flaws in the tax system distort incentives and retard U.S. economic growth. The result was to help create a climate of opinion in which supply-side economists could advocate radical tax cuts, leading to the massive budget deficits that Feldstein took the lead in denouncing. In the late 1970s and early 1980s a group of international economists—myself among them—similarly worked to persuade the economics profession that the principles of international trade needed to be rethought. This rethinking of international trade has won tenure and academic prestige for its leaders. But an unintended by-prod-

uct of the effort has been to lend some new intellectual respectability to protectionism.[8]

Traditional international economics attributes international trade
to underlying differences among countries. Australia exports wool
because its lands are well suited to sheep grazing, Thailand exports
labor-intensive manufactures because of its abundance of labor,
and so on. The new international economics, while not denying the
importance of this traditional view, adds that much international
trade also reflects national advantages that are created by historical
circumstance, and that then persist or grow because of other
advantages to large scale either in development or production. For
example, the development effort required to launch a new pas-
senger jet aircraft is so large that the world market will support only
one or two profitable firms. Once the United States had a head start
in producing aircraft, its position as the world's leading exporter
became self-reinforcing. So if you want to explain why the U.S.
exports aircraft, you should not look for underlying aspects of the
U.S. economy; you should study the historical circumstances that
gave the United States a head start in the industry.

Why does this provide a potential justification for protectionism?
Because if the pattern of international trade and specialization
largely reflects historical circumstances rather than underlying national strengths, then government policies can *in principle* shape
this pattern to benefit their domestic economies. As journalist
James Fallows put it in a recent plea for a more aggressive U.S. trade

---

8. The "new international economics" is generally associated with several
people: Princeton's Avinash Dixit, Tel Aviv's Elhanan Helpman, James
Brander and Barbara Spencer of the University of British Columbia, and
myself. The most widely read summary of the new ideas is a book I edited,
Strategic Trade Policy and the New International Economics (MIT Press, 1986);
a much more technical exposition is my *Rethinking International Trade* (MIT
Press, 1990).

policy, "Countries that try to promote higher-value, higher-tech industries will eventually have more of them than countries that don't."

Which industries should a country try to promote? One criterion is the potential for technological spillovers. Suppose that you believe that whichever country develops a high-definition television (HDTV) industry will find that its other industries, such as computers and semiconductors, gain an edge over their foreign competitors from their close contact with HDTV producers. Then it might be worth developing an HDTV sector—even if it requires a continuing subsidy due to costs that are persistently above those of foreign imports. This is an old argument, but it becomes much more attractive if the new theory is right, because the new theory suggests that the need for subsidy may be only temporary: Because comparative advantage is often created, not given, a temporary subsidy can lead to a permanent industry.

Another potential criterion for industry targeting has a sexy name: "strategic trade policy" (a term that is also loosely used to refer to the technological argument). A hypothetical example may convey its essence. Imagine that there is some good that could be developed and sold either by an American or a European firm. If either firm developed the product alone, it could earn large profits; however, the development costs are large enough that if both firms tried to enter the market, both would lose money. Which firm will actually enter? The answer may be determined by government intervention. If European governments subsidize their firm, or make it clear that it will have a protected domestic market, they may ensure that their firm enters while deterring the U.S. firm—and thereby also ensure that Europe, not America, gets the monopoly profits.

The strategic trade policy story (using the term to refer to both arguments) is not, at base, an argument for protectionism per se. It is really an argument for a limited government industrial policy consisting of carefully targeted subsidies, not for tariffs and import quotas. Yet it provides advocates of protectionism with a new intellectual gloss to justify their position, and it has been picked up enthusiastically by advocates of "managed trade" like Clyde Prestowitz and Robert Kuttner. If they do not argue that the United States should adopt a strategic trade policy, they at least claim that other countries—primarily Japan—have already done so, and that the United States needs to respond. As Kuttner puts it, "the New View radically alters the context of debate, for it removes the premise that nations such as Japan which practice strategic trade could not, by definition, be improving their welfare." There is a strong temptation for both politicians and intellectuals to run with this, to claim that all the old ideas about free trade should be thrown out the window.

In fact, however, none of the international economists responsible for the new trade theory has come out as an advocate of Kuttnerian trade policy. This is not because they are afraid to break the free-trade ranks. It is because the actual prospects for a successful strategic trade policy are not very good.

Once again, this is partly a matter of economics, partly one of politics. On the purely economic side, there just isn't any evidence that an aggressive strategic trade policy can produce large gains. Technological spillovers could be important, but they are difficult to measure. Take the example of HDTV. Many regard it as "one of the most, if not the most, crucial technological advancements" about to take place.[9] But a recent Congressional Budget Office study concluded that "it is hard to believe that HDTV will... play a pivotal role in the competitiveness and technological development of the electronics sector. . . ." Never mind which side is right:

---

9. Statement by Senator John Glenn (D-OH).

Someone is very wrong. Reaching a practical consensus on which sectors really are strategic is certain to be extremely difficult—even without the interjection of interest-group politics.

As for the possibility of capturing monopoly profits through strategic trade policy, the result of a good deal of technical analysis of the prospects for such policy in particular industries over the past few years is fairly discouraging. The general conclusion of those who have tried to estimate the likely gains from strategic trade policies is that, while you can do better than free trade, the potential net gains are nothing to write home about—they are even smaller than the conventional estimates of the costs of protection. For example, a recent simulation study of the prospects for strategic trade policies in a number of British industries by Anthony Venables of Southampton University found that the potential net gains were generally less than 3 percent of sales.

Meanwhile, there is political reality to consider. Given the uncertainty about what strategic trade policy should be, wouldn't any attempt at doing it turn into thinly disguised interest-group politics? Almost surely it would.

The protectionist prospect

There is a better intellectual case for protection than there used to be, and the case for free trade is often overstated. Nonetheless, there is still a good case for free trade as a general policy—not as an absolute ideal, but as a reasonable rule of thumb. American interests would probably best be served by a world of free trade, with the temptations of strategic trade policy kept out of reach by international treaty. Unfortunately, that's not going to happen, for two reasons.

First, the other major players *are* engaging in strategic trade policy. Quite possibly they are doing themselves more harm than good. But it is extremely difficult to maintain a hands-off position in the United States when other countries do not do the same, especially when America is evidently in relative decline. The extent to which other countries are using strategic policy shouldn't be overstated, but the examples—Japanese protection of supercomputers, European promotion of aircraft—are too conspicuous to dismiss.

Second, the politics of free trade depends on a belief that market access is reciprocal—that open U.S. markets can be traded for open markets elsewhere. For most U.S. trade this has been and remains true. When we negotiated a free trade pact with Canada, it meant increased access for both sides; the same would be true if we could negotiate a similar pact with Germany, or even with Mexico. But free trade becomes very difficult to sustain politically if there is a widespread and growing perception that one of the main players is following different rules.

The problem of relations with Japan—the second largest market economy, one of America's principal trading partners, but an economy into which the United States finds it difficult either to export or invest—is not the most important issue we face, but it is one of the hardest to solve.

10   Japan

An editorial page cartoon in 1987 showed a teacher addressing his history class. "Ironically," says the teacher in the first panel, "during the Second World War we were cooperating with the Soviet Union and fighting with Japan. . . ." In the second panel he continues, ". . . just like today."

It is easy to overstate the seriousness of the tension between the United States and Japan. When Wall Street economist Gary Shilling talks of a shift from Star Wars to Trade Wars, he is making a poor analogy: Trade conflict is a lot less serious than an arms race, let alone a shooting war. Still, the rising hostility of the American public to Japan, and the growing scorn of the Japanese for the United States, will almost surely be the biggest strain on world economic cooperation over the next decade.

Why are the United States and Japan at odds? In many ways the two countries have an economic relationship that provides great mutual benefits. Ask the Washington State loggers who sell their lumber to Japan at twice the price it would fetch on the domestic market, or the U.S. Treasury, which would have to pay far higher rates on the national debt if it were not for the inflow of Japanese capital; and, on the other side, ask Honda, which has half its market in America, or the managers of Japanese pension funds, who get a better return on U.S. bonds than they could get at home.

Yet there is a growing sense among many Americans that Japan is playing the global economic game by different rules from the rest of us. As long as the United States had a comfortable economic and technological superiority over Japan, complaints about Japan were limited to a small group, easily dismissed as representatives of special interests. But with Japan now overtaking the United States in one field after another, the previous murmur of complaint has become a loud clamor.

Meanwhile, the Japanese view it all as simple envy and an attempt to make excuses. They see America as a failing economic power, its competitiveness crippled by social disintegration, racial diversity, poor education, lazy workers, a pervasive emphasis on short-term gains, and a general intellectual and moral flabbiness. To the Japanese, U.S. trade complaints are an attempt to blame our own problems on someone else; their initial dismay has turned into growing anger, and they are increasingly coming to despise us.

Here in America, the lines are already being drawn. A 1989 *Newsweek* story on Japan divided American experts into "apologists" and "bashers"—no middle ground.

But what is the truth? A first step is to ask what is really true about Japan. Only then can we look for answers to the growing tension in U.S.-Japan relations.

The Japanese difference

Does Japan really play by different rules? You might think that this would be a simple question of fact, but it isn't. Instead, it is a source of bitter dispute.

The reason is that there is a wide disparity between the letter of the law and what actually seems to happen in Japan. On paper, Japan's markets are fairly open. Japan is openly and outrageously protectionist when it comes to agricultural goods—everyone knows about the prices of beef and rice.[10] On manufactured goods, however, Japan's tariff rates are about the same as those of other industrial countries, and Japan has few of the "voluntary export restraints" and "orderly marketing agreements" that limit imports of autos, steel, and other goods in both the United States and Europe. So in international discussions of trade policy, Japanese officials can describe their nation with a straight face as a leading practitioner of free trade.

There's only one thing wrong with this picture: If Japan is so open to the world, how come nobody can sell there?

By now, everyone has heard the anecdotes of businessmen trying to sell goods in Japan—of firms that politely refuse to consider your product, even if it is better and cheaper than the local alternative, of retailers who will not distribute foreign goods. These anecdotes come mostly from interested parties, and they might be dismissed as sour grapes if the overall evidence did not bear them out. For the simple fact is that Japan spends less than half as much of its income on imports of manufactured goods as any other advanced nation.

It is important to point out that we are *not* talking about the fact that Japan runs a large trade surplus in manufactures. Trade surpluses are ultimately determined by the balance between domestic saving and investment. Japan runs a large manufactures surplus because it has a very high savings rate, and also because it *must* run a surplus in manufactures to offset its imports of raw materials. But it's not the size of the surplus that makes people accuse Japan of foul play; it's the way that surplus is achieved, with Japan seemingly a country that exports but does not import.

---

10. Although it is surprisingly hard to get Japanese to admit even this. I have had the experience of finding Japanese economists from the private sector refuse to acknowledge that the rice policy is costly, even in informal conversation. When pressed hard, they explained that they did not feel it was their place to criticize their government to a foreigner.

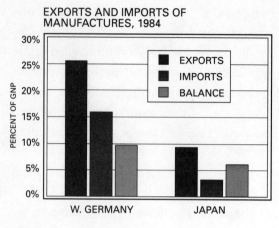

EXPORTS AND IMPORTS OF
MANUFACTURES, 1984

Figure 22
Measured as a share of national income, Germany actually runs substantially
larger surpluses in its trade in manufactured goods than does Japan.

A revealing comparison can be made between Japan and West
Germany, the third largest market economy. In many ways Japan
and Germany have similar economies. Both are high-saving countries that export large amounts of capital to the rest of the world.
Both are also crowded countries, with few raw materials, that must
run trade surpluses in manufactures simply to pay for their food
and oil. And both have run very large trade surpluses in manufacturing in recent years. In fact, as Figure 22 shows, Germany's trade
surplus in manufactures is actually larger as a share of its GNP than
Japan's.

But there the resemblance ends. Germany is one of the world's
greatest markets for imported manufactured goods. The trade surplus comes about only because exports are even larger. Germany
simply trades more, in both directions. Whatever complaints one
may hear about German economic policy, neither the Americans
nor their fellow Europeans accuse the Germans of having a tacitly
closed market.

The Japanese and some of their defenders (like economist Gary Saxonhouse) will reply that the difference is geography: Germany trades so much because it is in the middle of Europe, while Japan is isolated at the edge of Asia. There is some point to this, though with modern transportation and communications distance is not what it used to be. Even allowing for geography, however, careful analysis of Japan's trade volume suggests that it imports only about half as much as one would expect.[11] The businessman's complaint that the Japanese will not import anything they can make themselves is an exaggeration, yet the overall evidence broadly supports it.

But what limits imports into Japan, when there are only low tariffs and few import quotas? At this point the Japan experts get all fuzzy—which is probably appropriate, because Japan is a fuzzy kind of society, without the hard-edged legalisms that Americans, in particular, expect. Japan hands point to the interlocking structure of ownership within Japan; to the long-term relationships between suppliers, distributors, and banks; to an economy that resembles an elaborate old boys' network more than the free-wheeling markets of America (and which is rife with practices that would be illegal under U.S. antitrust law). For any outsider, this economic structure is hard to break into; for foreigners, it is particularly difficult.

Some foreign experts like to view the Japanese system as not just closed but conspiratorial, tacitly directed by top officials at the Ministry of International Trade and Industry (MITI) and the Ministry of Finance. This is the view advanced by such bashers as Clyde Prestowitz, whose book *Trading Places* portrays a systematic Japa-

---

11. The decisive salvo in the academic debate was a 1987 paper on Japanese imports by Robert Lawrence of the Brookings Institution, which showed to the satisfaction of many economists that Japan really does have unexpectedly small imports. It is a measure of the growing polarization in the U.S. debate that *Newsweek* classes Lawrence, who has been an active crusader for free trade, as a "basher."

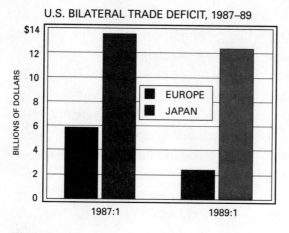

Figure 23
The dollar's fall, which helped the United States to cut its trade deficit with
Europe, has had little impact on its deficit with Japan.

nese pursuit of strategic advantage at America's expense. It is also
a view that is increasingly out of date.

There is no question that before the early 1970s the Japanese
system was heavily directed from the top, with MITI and the
Ministry of Finance influencing the allocation of credit and foreign
exchange in an effort to push the economy where they liked. For a
long time, however, Japanese firms have had plenty of cash on
hand, both foreign and domestic, and a correspondingly greater
ability to ignore suggestions from above. Old habits of deference to
central authority are still around, but the still popular image of a
centralized "Japan Inc." is at least 15 years behind the times.
Fashionable current descriptions of Japan, like the recent book of
Karel van Wolferen, depict an economy that is characterized neither by free competition nor by central direction, but rather by a
web of personal ties and long-term understandings—a conspiracy,
if you like, but one without leaders.

Even if there are no central strategists, however, the Japanese
economy often appears to be following the very type of strategic

trade policy that some Americans would like to see adopted here. The ranks of Japanese firms seem to close most strongly against imports of goods that embody new technologies, like supercomputers or what is known in electronics jargon as "amorphous materials." When imports into Japan do increase, as they have since the yen began to rise in 1985, they tend to be either unsophisticated goods or products of the overseas affiliates of Japanese firms, and not the kinds of goods that American firms think they should be able to sell. It is revealing that the falling dollar had a marked effect in shrinking the U.S. trade deficit with Europe but hardly any effect on our deficit with Japan, even though the dollar fell more against the yen than against any other currency.

CORPORATE TAXATION AND FOREIGN DIRECT INVESTMENT

Somewhat surprisingly, the tax reform of 1986, which, in effect, increased the rate of taxation on corporations, may have been one of the factors that led to a shift of Japanese investment away from passive portfolio investments and toward the direct acquisition of U.S. firms.

In 1981, the United States offered very generous depreciation allowances that cut effective corporate tax rates sharply. Somewhat paradoxically, this acted as a disincentive for Japanese firms to own U.S. corporations. When a Japanese firm owns a U.S. corporation, it must eventually pay taxes to the Japanese government on any profits its subsidiary sends home—with a credit for taxes paid to the U.S. government. This meant that Japanese-owned firms, unlike U.S.-owned firms, could not realize the full benefits of the lower tax rate, since the gain from the lower tax rate here was partially offset by the reduced tax credit at home. Thus the low corporate tax rates of 1981-1986 had the effect of making corporations more valuable in U.S. than in Japanese hands.

The 1986 tax reform, which raised the effective corporate tax rate, eliminated this bias toward domestic ownership, and may therefore have played a role in the surge of Japanese acquisitions of U.S. firms that followed.

In sum, then, the widespread perception that Japan plays by different rules is basically right. This is not a moral judgment; it's not a question of what's right or what's fair. It is just a statement of fact. Japan's market is not open to foreigners in the way that U.S. or German markets are open.

The Japanese are coming!

As trade conflict between the U.S. and Japan grew in the mid-1980s, U.S. officials tried to buy time, hoping that a fall in the dollar eventually would take the pressure off. As it turned out, however, the lower dollar, while quite effective elsewhere, had virtually no effect on U.S.-Japan trade. And partly as a result, a new source of tension has arisen: Japanese direct investment in the United States.

Japan has been investing heavily abroad, largely in the United States, since 1982—a net capital outflow that is the inevitable counterpart of Japan's balance-of-payments surpluses. Until 1986, the Japanese characteristically put their money into "portfolio" investments that yielded income but not control: Treasury bills, corporate paper, and minority stock positions. Then, for reasons that are still controversial, they changed their approach. Even as the overall rate of Japanese investment abroad tapered off, more and more of it took the form of foreign direct investment: investment aimed at establishing operational control. The purchase of Columbia Pictures by Sony made headlines, but it was just one conspicuous example of a broad trend.

The numbers show the trend clearly. As recently as 1985, Japan parked three-quarters of its foreign investment in passive sources of income; now two-thirds of its investment flows are used to acquire or extend control. The United States, as the world's leading capital importer, has provided the counterpart: Where in the early days of our trade deficit we were able to finance it mostly by selling

COMPOSITION OF JAPANESE INVESTMENT FLOW

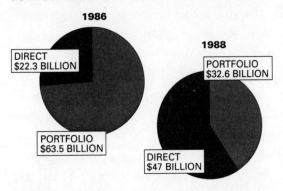

Figure 24
Since 1986 Japan has increasingly used its accumulation of assets abroad not simply to yield returns but also to buy control.

debt, we now sell whole firms. Many of these sales are to countries other than Japan—British direct investment is still larger than that of Japan—but Japanese firms in the United States have been growing rapidly.

Why is this happening now? One reason is the fall in the dollar, which has made the cash resources of Japanese firms look large relative to the prices of U.S. firms. The tax reform act of 1986 may also have inadvertently opened the floodgates. (See box, page 121.) Also, sheer herd instinct may have played a role: Once a few Japanese firms had shown the way, others rushed to follow.

The more important question is whether it is anything to worry about. Twenty years ago, when U.S. multinational corporations were growing in Europe, many Europeans feared that the "American challenge" would overwhelm them. In the end, U.S. investment in Europe did not grow without limit, and U.S. firms in Europe soon came to be regarded as perfectly acceptable corporate citizens. Won't the same turn out to be true of Japanese firms in the United States?

Well, maybe. But here as elsewhere Japan looks different, enough so to cause some worries. If you want to find cause for alarm about the Japanese invasion, there are two facts that can give the complacent pause. First, while Japanese firms invest abroad, Japan itself seems to be a very hard place in which to invest—so Japanese firms may have a strategic advantage over their foreign rivals in the form of a protected home base. Second, Japanese firms in the U.S. appear to behave differently from other firms.

The apparent inability of foreign firms to operate on a large scale in Japan is an even more striking fact than Japan's resistance to imports. Figure 25 compares the role of foreign-owned firms in Japan with their role in other advanced countries. Europeans have long been accustomed to the idea of working for foreign employers, having a substantial part of the capital stock foreign-owned, and so on; with growing foreign direct investment in the United States, America increasingly looks similar. But Japan is barely touched by foreign firms.

SHARE OF FOREIGN-OWNED FIRMS, 1986

Figure 25
Foreign-owned firms now play an important role in all major industrial countries—except Japan, where their role remains of minimal importance.

Japan's situation with regard to direct investment is like its situation with regard to imports, only more so. *De jure*, Japan is wide open; while the government does have some power to block foreign investments, that power is rarely used. *De facto*, foreign firms in Japan face endless informal obstacles.

The point is that with Japan now one of the world's great economic powers, the asymmetry of access—Japanese firms can invest abroad, but foreign firms find it difficult to invest in Japan—gives firms of Japanese origin a kind of strategic advantage that is not negligible.

But what difference does it make? Why not accept Japanese firms abroad?

The first wave of Japanese direct investment in the United States saw the creation of manufacturing subsidiaries—first in color televisions, then in autos. To optimists, these investments seemed a clear plus from an American point of view: new plants, new jobs, domestic production in place of imports. Admittedly, there was always a concern that Japanese production would displace domestic autos instead of imports; but on the whole most people looked favorably on these "greenfield" investments.

The wave of investment since 1986 has not, however, followed this earlier model. The Japanese have not for the most part been building new plants. Instead, they have been acquiring existing U.S. enterprises. Bridgestone, a Japanese firm, bought Firestone; Sony bought Columbia Pictures. When a Japanese firm buys an existing American firm, we have to ask whether that firm will be run differently, and if so, whether the U.S. economy will be hurt or helped by the difference.

The optimistic view is that the Japanese will buy firms that they know they can run better than the original management, and so the result will be an increase in efficiency. The Japanese auto companies

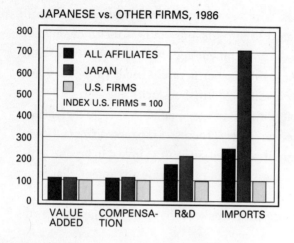

Figure 26
Japanese-owned firms in the United States look similar to U.S.-owned firms and firms owned by other countries in terms of value-added per worker, wages, and spending on R&D. However, they have a much higher tendency to buy inputs from abroad.

have shown that they can run plants in the United States at Japanese levels of productivity, raising the efficiency of the U.S. labor force both directly and by shaming Detroit into doing better. Surely they will do the same in other industries, and to that extent will help the U.S. economy (although whether Japanese firms can improve the management of the motion picture industry is fairly doubtful).

The pessimistic view is that the Japanese will rearrange their firms to suit Japanese interests, at U.S. expense. Prestowitz and Robert Reich predict that the Japanese will keep the high-wage activities, the R&D, and much of the sourcing of parts in Japan. The United States, in this view, will be left with "screwdriver" plants where low-wage American workers assemble Japanese products.

Since the great wave of Japanese investment is so recent, it is too early to tell how it will turn out. The behavior of the Japanese firms already here, however, suggests that they are innocent of two of the charges, but guilty of the third. As Figure 26 shows, Japanese firms already here actually pay wages as high or higher than both American firms and other foreign firms in the United States; they also do just as much R&D. Unfortunately, the third charge is true: Japanese firms do seem to import a lot more, most of it presumably from Japanese suppliers, than either U.S. firms or other foreign firms. On average, foreign firms in the United States import more than twice as much per worker as American firms; Japanese firms import well over twice as much as the average foreign firm.

It is possible to make excuses for this high propensity to import. In particular, the imports of Japanese subsidiaries may reflect their sheer newness, the lack of time to build up a local supply network. On the other hand, a tendency to buy from their regular suppliers, even when it might be cheaper to source locally, is just what one would expect given the other things we know about Japanese industry. (Some recent comparisons of the behavior of Japanese firms in Australia with those from other countries reveal the same Japanese reluctance to buy either locally or on the world market.)

So here is the case against Japanese multinationals, if you want to make it: They have a strategic advantage against the rest of the world because of their protected home base, and they use this advantage to pursue a buy-Japanese policy even when they acquire production facilities abroad. Perhaps the advantages of attracting Japanese firms outweigh these complaints. But in the highly charged atmosphere of the 1990s it is inevitable that Japanese investment will draw the same kind of lightning as Japanese trade— and perhaps more so.

How much of a problem is it?

During the 1970s it was popular for radicals both in the Third World and in the United States to blame the industrial nations, and America in particular, for the backwardness of the rest of the world.

Someone once wrote of these radicals that they seemed to see America as a kind of spacecraft, shooting death rays at the Third World's economy. Few people would now portray the United States that way, but increasingly that is the way Americans seem to view Japan.

How much of a problem does "the Japanese difference" pose for the United States? To defenders of Japan, and to those who believe that a restructured American economy is about to enter a golden age, there is no problem at all. To alarmists like Prestowitz, Japan's challenge is undermining America's economic prospects. The reality is more mundane. The Japanese difference hurts the American economy, but only a little. If our prospects are not too good, the fault lies not in Tokyo but in Washington and New York. The Japan problem is real, but it is not central.

The reason is simple. The main thing that matters for American living standards is still our own productivity. Foreign trade and foreign competition can only make a difference at the margin. If Japan's economy were more open, if Japanese firms abroad were better local citizens, we might be able to trade U.S. goods and services for imports at better terms. Our real income would therefore be higher. But it would be only a marginal improvement. The reasons for our disappointing economic performance lie overwhelmingly in our own shortcomings.

The flip side is also true: Japan's success does not in any important way rest on predatory behavior against the rest of the world. Japan saves six times as high a fraction of its income as the United States and educates its children better than we do. This year Japanese industry will invest more in total than U.S. industry, even though Japan has only half our population. These are sufficient reasons for Japan to grow far faster than the United States, whatever our trading relations. Indeed, it is worth remembering that Japan's economy is not, popular myth to the contrary, primarily an export machine: Japan exports only 14 percent of what it produces, less than any other major industrial country except the United States. It is no wonder that the Japanese are scornful of Americans who want to claim that Japan's success is somehow "stolen" at America's expense.

So it is important to keep a sense of perspective about the Japan problem. Japan is not our nemesis. Japan's success hurts our pride far more than it hurts our standard of living.

Yet there is still a Japan problem. Japan is a great economic power that does not play by the same rules as the other great economic powers. Economically and, above all, politically, that is a fact that cannot be ignored. One way or another, the United States has got to find a way of dealing with Japan.

What to do

There are two extreme views about what to do about Japan. On one side are the old-time free traders, who want us in effect to turn the other cheek. On the other side are the bashers, who want us to confront Japan and demand massive change, or else. So emotional has the dispute between these factions become that it has descended to the level of *ad hominem* charges—free traders accused of getting money from the Japanese, bashers accused of getting money from protectionist special interests. But let's look at the case on the merits.

The free traders—led by economists like Herbert Stein of the American Enterprise Institute and Jagdish Bhagwati of Columbia University—start with the general presumption that free trade is the best economic policy for a country, whatever the rest of the world does. There is an old saw in trade theory: Saying that my country should be protectionist because other countries are is like saying that, because other countries have rocky coasts, I should block up my own harbors. They predict that any kind of confrontation with Japan will end up delivering U.S. trade policy into the hands of our own special interest groups who will wrap their selfish demands in the flag. These free traders also either discount the claims that Japan's *de jure* open markets are not open *de facto,* or adopt the legal view that internal institutional arrangements are not the business of trade law. They then argue that the United States should see to it that our own trade is as free as possible, urge other countries to do the same, and then sit back and enjoy the benefits.

The bashers, of course, view it all very differently. They see large costs to America from the asymmetry with Japan. While their gut feelings may come from conventional mercantilist sentiments, the more sophisticated bashers have learned to employ some of the modern arguments against unilateral free trade that are now current in economic theory. And the bashers therefore call for presentation of an ultimatum to Japan: Change your ways, or else!

For those in neither camp, the whole issue is agonizing. The old-time free trade position seems naive, reflecting neither the realities of Japan nor the political possibilities for America. Yet the basher program seems equally unappealing. Above all, it is virtually certain to fail in its premise: Japan will not suddenly change, and we will therefore be stuck with the "or else."

The point is that if Japan is a conspiracy, it is not a centrally directed one. There is no small group of men in Tokyo who can deliver a liberal Japanese trading regime over the course of a couple of years. Americans often find it hard to believe that Japan is a real country, with real politics, where the average member of parliament is much more concerned with pleasing his constituents (and his campaign contributors) than with keeping America mollified.

So the end result of any attempt to force a radical opening of Japan's markets with the threat of U.S. protectionism will be either an embarrassing and politically costly retreat or a situation in which we must carry out our threat. Down that road lies the prospect of a fragmentation of the world into mutually protectionist trading blocs—a costly outcome though not a tragic one.

Is there a middle way? Perhaps not. It seems likely that the bashers will more or less have their way, and that this decade will be one of growing economic nationalism.

My own proposal is that we adopt an explicit, but limited, U.S. industrial policy. That is, the U.S. government should make a decision to frankly subsidize a few sectors, especially in the high-technology area, that may plausibly be described as "strategic," where there is a perceived threat from Japanese competition. It is possible that the costs of such a policy would exceed its economic benefits. But the downside would be limited: Federal expenditures of, say, $10 billion a year to support industrial R&D consortia would produce at least some benefits. So at worst the net cost of the program to the economy would be a few billion dollars a year—or less than one-tenth of 1 percent of GNP.

A limited industrial policy of this sort would also serve two important political purposes: answering those who fear that Japanese strategic trade policy is squeezing the United States out of crucial economic sectors; and providing an incentive for the Japanese to find ways to open up their system—if only to persuade the United States not to subsidize industries that compete with Japanese exports. Moreover, an on-budget program would be less likely to become a special-interest pork barrel than a program of "managed trade," where the costs consist of higher prices that are virtually invisible to consumers.

It is important to emphasize that I am *not* advocating some form of managed trade—nor would managed trade be an acceptable second best alternative to this sort of limited industrial policy. One of the main purposes of this proposal is precisely to provide an alternative to managed trade, with its hidden costs and near-total dominance by interest-group politics.

Viewed from the right perspective, then, a limited U.S. industrial policy could be a relatively cheap way to cope with the stresses produced by relative U.S. decline and the special problem of dealing with Japan. It is unlikely, however, that such a clean solution will be adopted. Instead, the political system is much more likely to adopt some form of "managed trade" via import quotas. Bashers like Kuttner prefer managed trade, perhaps because its costs are less identifiable than straightforward subsidies; politicians prefer it for the same reason. And in the current political environment anything that raises the current budget deficit is avoided whatever its future costs.

IV
Financial Follies

In many ways the American economy since the mid-1980s has been remarkably placid. Following the severe recession of the decade's early years, growth has been steady, unemployment has gradually declined, inflation has been relatively flat. After a dizzying rise in the early and mid-1980s, both the trade and budget deficits stabilized, then turned modestly down. For the average American it has been a calm if not exactly a prosperous period.

Yet for those who make their living from financial markets, the 1980s were anything but a quiet time. The volume of transactions on world markets has swelled to unprecedented levels. There is now more trading of foreign exchange on a typical day than there was in a month ten years ago. The ups and downs of financial markets of the 1980s rival or surpass anything seen before: The 1987 stock market crash was bigger and more global than the Great Crash of 1929; the decline of the dollar from 1985 to 1987 was one of the biggest devaluations ever experienced by an industrial country not wracked by high inflation.

Why has the world of finance become so hyperactive? There is no single answer. Yet much of the explanation surely lies in the same persistence of trade deficits and especially inflation that has preoccupied economic policy. Inflation, for instance, has gradually undermined some traditional economic institutions. The rise of inflation essentially bankrupted a large number of savings and loans—

and Washington's failure to face up to this fact turned what was a relatively modest problem into a fiscal nightmare. The rise of inflation also encouraged Third World nations to acquire large foreign debts, which became insupportable as inflation came down. And persistent inflation, interacting with the tax system, encouraged corporations to replace equity with debt—a process bound up with the boom in takeovers and buyouts, and with the restructuring of the economy that the trade deficits helped make necessary.

The torrid financial markets of the 1980s, then, were one of the main consequences of the unresolved business of economic policy. At the same time, they did much to define the style and image of the decade, by creating a new class of sudden rich. Indeed, never in modern history has so much money been made by so few people in so little time.

To complete our picture of the American economy, we need to look at three scenes from the financial world: the savings and loan affair, in which seemingly technical policy issues turned into a financial mess of startling size; the Third World debt problem, which is greatly overrated as a U.S. economic issue; and the takeover and buyout boom, which is probably what the decade will ultimately be remembered for.

11   The Savings & Loan
Scandal

The conservative economic program launched by Ronald Reagan in the 1980s had two main elements. One was lower taxes; the other was deregulation—getting the government out of the private sector's way. While most economists were skeptical about the effectiveness of tax cuts for stimulating the economy, deregulation commanded wide support. Even liberal economists were persuaded by the arguments of reformers that everyone could gain from deregulation of airlines, trucking, and banking.

Yet the biggest single economic policy disaster of the 1980s sprang from a misguided attempt at deregulation. Deregulation of the savings and loan industry turned what might have been a $15 billion problem at the beginning of the decade into a burden on the taxpayers at least 10 and perhaps 20 times as great by the decade's end. Of course, the reasons for this debacle went deeper than simple misguided deregulatory zeal. But the rhetoric of economic freedom helped mask what might otherwise have been seen as an obviously irresponsible policy.

Origins of the crisis

Once upon a time, there was a staid, familiar institution called a savings and loan. Savings and loans were created to give ordinary people a safe way to store their money while earning modest interest. To secure the safety of this money, S&L deposits were insured by a Federal agency, the Federal Savings and Loan Insurance Corporation, or FSLIC.

From the beginning, it was realized that insuring deposits created a potential source of risk and corruption. A banker whose deposits are publicly insured does not have to prove that his bank is sound. If he offers potential depositors an interest rate that is just slightly above the market rate, they will put their money in his bank, no questions asked—for they know that they cannot lose their money.

But a license to borrow as much as you like, at a fixed interest rate, is a license to gamble. Open a savings and loan; offer an interest rate a little above going rates to attract a lot of deposits; and invest the money you get in the riskiest projects you can find. If the projects work out, great—you've made a lot of money. If not, and the bank does not have enough money to repay its depositors—well, that's FSLIC's problem, not yours. It's heads you win, tails the taxpayers lose. Without the insurance, of course, your depositors would want to check on what kind of investments you were making, and if they thought you were taking too many risks, they would refuse to put money in your bank. With the insurance, they don't care.

This is an obvious problem, and until 1981 it was met with the obvious answer: eligible investments were tightly regulated and individual S&Ls were regularly audited. Lending was largely restricted to homebuyers under rules designed to prevent excessive risk taking. It was an exchange of a privilege (deposit insurance) for a responsibility (low-risk investing). And until the mid-1970s it worked quite well.

What went wrong was a risk that nobody had counted on: inflation. During the 1970s, inflation soared, and market interest rates rose along with it. At first, savings and loans simply lost depositors as the interest rates they paid grew less and less competitive with those offered by banks and money market funds. This problem was solved by allowing S&Ls to pay higher rates, but this only created a new problem. To hold their depositors, S&Ls were obliged to pay interest rates of 8, 9, or 10 percent. Meanwhile, their assets consisted of 30-year home loans made at 4, 5, or 6 percent in the days before inflation began to climb. Instead of lending out money at a higher rate than they paid on deposits, which is what banks are supposed to do, S&Ls found themselves paying more on deposits than they were earning on their assets. By 1980 many S&Ls were clearly in danger of going bankrupt.

Under the rules of the game that were supposed to be in place, this was where FSLIC was expected to do its job. Through nobody's fault, many S&Ls had made investments that in retrospect were a mistake. The solution? Shut them down, pay off their depositors, and let FSLIC cover the difference between what they had and their obligations. Estimates by economists like Robert Litan of the Brookings Institution suggest that about $15 billion in Federal money would have allowed the liquidation of those S&Ls that were in real trouble, and thus ended the story.

But that's not what happened.

Double or nothing, 1981–89

The S&L story after 1980 is a simple one. Neither Congress nor the Administration wanted to swallow the cost of shutting down bankrupt S&Ls. So they elected to play double or nothing: to offer the entire S&L industry a more favorable deal in return for staying in business, hoping that the problem would go away. Instead, predictably, the problem got worse.

That's not how it was portrayed at the time, of course. The ostensible purpose of the change in the rules announced in 1981 was to allow S&Ls to make more productive use of their money by substantially deregulating the investments they could make—a change justified on the general principle of free markets. But a real move to free markets would have removed the privilege of deposit insurance as the price of deregulation of investment. What the thrifts got, instead, was freedom without responsibility. They now had the right to make risky investments, while continuing to be able to assure depositors that their money was guaranteed by the Federal government.

In the short run, this worked. S&Ls received a new injection of capital from high-roller entrepreneurs who were willing to maintain payments to depositors in exchange for the opportunity to gamble with their money. And S&Ls either became risk takers or were bought by men who were. All across the country savings and loans became financiers of speculative developments, projects that could conceivably make a lot of money but were more likely to lose it.

If the economy had boomed through the whole decade, if oil prices had stayed high, if real interest rates had not risen so much, it is just possible that this game of double or nothing might have worked. But, instead, oil prices collapsed, taking the price of Texas real estate with them, and the economy passed through a massive recession. Even after the recovery real interest rates remained much higher than before. By 1989 the S&Ls were in far worse shape than they had been in 1981; closing down the really troubled ones would now cost at least $166 billion. Even allowing for inflation, the real burden to the taxpayers was at least six times as high as it would have been had the S&L problem been dealt with at the beginning of decade.

Apportioning the blame

When the size of the S&L mess became apparent, sensational stories about the abuses of the 1980s hit the press. Tales of bank owners living high at the bank's expense, of corrupt deals, of wild risk-taking made exciting reading. Yet it is not clear that the American public has absorbed the real story of what happened.

Reading the press accounts, one might imagine that what happened was some kind of mysterious invasion of immoral men— Jimmy Stewarts run out of their offices by conniving J. R. Ewings. Many of the press stories, aside from moralizing, placed the blame on the regulators for failing to keep an eye on their charges. And surely there was plenty of both corruption and malfeasance. But emphasizing these misses the point, just as focusing on the evil of the Medellín cartel misses the point of the drug problem. The great bulk of the losses came from taking bad risks, not from literal theft. And besides, Americans in general are neither better nor worse people than they used to be. So the real question has to be: What made socially destructive behavior in this industry so much more attractive than it used to be?

We already know the answer. The partial deregulation of the early 1980s made it possible for S&Ls to gamble with their depositors' money, with the Federal government absorbing the risks. An S&L was worth more in the hands of a gambler than in the hands of a prudent business manager. So the owners of S&Ls either learned to be high-rollers, or were bought out by individuals who already were. Not surprisingly, the class of people who were temperamentally suited to take advantage of the opportunities offered by privilege without responsibility contained more than its share of rogues and criminals. Yet the epidemic of white-collar crime in the thrift industry was a result of the environment the government created, not an independent event.

Locking the barn door

Regulators, Congressional staffers, and economists have always known the answer to the savings and loan problem: Tighten the restrictions on the S&Ls, and require the owners to put in more capital if they want to stay in business. If the capital is not forthcoming, close them down (and pay off the depositors). This was the right answer even in 1980; it is even more obviously the right answer today.

Yet this obvious answer has been avoided by both the Administration and Congress for nearly a decade. Even the S&L bailout scheme negotiated in 1989 was only a partial fix: It left the capital requirements on the thrifts too low and failed to allocate enough money to close down all the institutions that need to be shut. This will stretch out the problem for years to come—and quite possibly cost the taxpayers scores of billions of dollars in avoidable future payments. The whole S&L story is one of almost incredibly irresponsible Federal policy, repeated year after year, and it still goes on.

Why? The U.S. government fell into two traps; it is hard to say which is the more disreputable.

First, any subsidy program, no matter how costly to the economy, creates a vested interest in its continuance. For most of the past decade there has existed a set of policies that allow shrewd operators to gamble with public funds; these operators are prepared to oppose the loss of their privileges. Given the style of the people who have come to populate the industry, they are also prepared to push their political case with a brashness and disregard for propriety that more established, genteel interest groups avoid. In the long run, the aggressiveness of the S&L industry undercuts its credibility, and threatens too many of its political allies with scandal. But the people we are talking about are not interested in the long run, and in the short run their lavishness can be effective. So the Federal government has created a sort of Frankenstein monster of political economy, which may still devour many billions of dollars before it is slain.

Second, shutting the S&Ls down costs money. Worse yet, even as the foolishness of going on with double or nothing has grown, the cost of stopping the game has risen—and the restraints of Federal budget cutting have grown. In the 1989 thrift plan the problem was finessed by putting the expenditures off-budget, but the trickery is straining the whole process.

What makes this sad is that paying off the depositors now is not really a cost to the taxpayers, because that cost has already been incurred. The real decision to spend taxpayer money was made long ago, when the Federal government chose to encourage risk taking by institutions whose downside was publicly insured. The real cost of that decision to the economy took place when the dubious investments made by these institutions went bad; paying the depositors off now is simply giving them money they already think they have. Paying the cost of closing the S&Ls now only recognizes these costs.

There is no case for putting off the inevitable—not even concern about national saving. Even if the Federal government must borrow the money with which to pay off the S&L depositors, it will not by any calculation have a negative effect on national saving. The depositors will not feel any richer—they thought they had that money anyway—so they will not increase their consumption. Meanwhile, by stopping the game, the Federal government will cut its future losses. This is a clear case where the efforts of the government to avoid increasing the *measured* deficit actually aggravate the problems that deficit reduction is supposed to cure.

During the 1970s, private bankers in the United States and elsewhere decided that lending to Third World countries was a good idea. Loans to governments, or loans guaranteed by governments, looked safe enough to the bankers to make the higher yields on Third World lending attractive—as Citibank's Walter Wriston asserted, in remarks he was later to regret, "Sovereign nations don't go bankrupt."

As long as the flow of money continued, everything looked fine: The debtor countries could pay interest and principal easily out of the new loans. In 1981 and 1982, however, for a variety of reasons, confidence evaporated, and the flow of money dried up with it—and it turned out that the countries could not generate enough cash to service their debt. The result was a rolling crisis that continues to this day.

Third World debt figures prominently in many pictures of the world economy at the end of the 1980s. In human terms this is clearly appropriate. Most of Latin America and most of Sub-Saharan Africa, as well as a few other nations like the Philippines, have been hard hit by the debt crisis. Economic growth in the highly indebted countries (HICs) has been far slower since 1981 than before. Unemployment and inflation have soared, living standards of already very poor families have deteriorated. For some of those at the bottom in Latin America (and even more so in Africa), the debt crisis has been lethal.

As a concern of U.S. *economic* policy, however, the debt crisis is not a major issue. The unfortunate fact about poor countries is that they don't have much money—and so, in purely economic terms, they do not carry much weight. The combined gross national products of all troubled debtors are less than 4 percent of the world's GNP. The total value of all loans to troubled debtors is less than 1 percent of the wealth of the creditor nations; the debt service on those loans less than one-quarter of 1 percent of the national incomes of the creditors. Terrible as it is to say, the United States does not have a strong economic interest in what happens to Third World debtors.

This observation can cut two ways. On one side, the U.S. government can, if it chooses, neglect or mishandle the debt situation with few domestic consequences. On the other hand, if Washington feels that it has a national security or humanitarian interest in seeing the debt burden reduced, it could accomplish this at a relatively low cost—in fact, a massive program of debt reduction could be carried out at a cost to U.S. taxpayers that is about one-twentieth that of the savings and loan bailout.

Before getting to this, however, let's look at the options.

Do we need a debt policy?

The United States and other creditor countries have never tried one option for dealing with Third World debt that in retrospect might not have been such a bad idea. This was to do nothing: to treat the whole affair as a private matter between banks and their clients. Instead, from the beginning the debt crisis has been a matter for continual high-level government intervention.

Why won't creditor countries leave the issue alone? There are three main answers.

First, there has been a long-standing fear that the debt crisis, if left unattended, could provoke a worldwide banking crisis on the 1931 model. In 1982, when the crisis broke, it was thought that widespread defaults might leave many of the world's major banks insolvent. In the modern world, with its elaborate bank regulation and supervision, this would not have closed the banks: It would have put them into government hands. But inadvertent nationalization of the banking industry was not a prospect the Reagan Administration welcomed. Today the risk of such an event is greatly reduced, primarily because banks have built up their capital as insurance against possible losses. Massive defaults on Third World debt would still put some banks under water—among major banks, analysts frequently cite Manufacturers Hanover as a problem case—but the kind of wholesale collapse of private banking that was feared in 1982 now seems improbable.

Second, the creditor nations felt that they had an interest in the political stability of debtors, and that a confrontation between debtors and bankers could lead to radicalization. In 1982 the picture of a leftist-populist movement rising to power in Mexico by denouncing foreign banks and demanding debt repudiation did not seem farfetched. Indeed, it is still a reasonable scenario—not for this year or next, but it would be foolish to dismiss it as a possibility for this century.

Third, officials at the Federal Reserve, the U.S. Treasury, and the International Monetary Fund believed that government leadership could fashion a better solution than private actors could achieve on their own.

Financing vs. forgiving

Suppose that someone who owes you money approaches you and tells you that he cannot pay in full. After checking out the story, you find that he is telling the truth, and that no purpose would be served by trying to force him to come up with the money. What do you do? You have two basic choices. You can give him time by postponing the payment, in effect lending him the money he cannot pay, and hope that he will be able to pay later. Or you can tell him to pay what he can, and consider the account settled (except that you probably will not lend him money again for a long time). The same basic options confront the creditors of the Third World: They can either *finance* the debt—that is, postpone the countries' obligations and hope that things will look better later on—or they can *forgive* it, reduce the debtors' obligations to a level that they may be able to pay.

From 1982 until 1989, official policy toward Third World debt was based on the premise that financing was enough, that if debtor nations were given time, they would eventually be able to meet their obligations. Then, in March 1989, Treasury Secretary Nicholas Brady declared that the United States was now advocating a strategy of debt reduction. Exactly how this is to be accomplished remains unclear, but it does seem as if the overall emphasis has shifted from financing to forgiving.

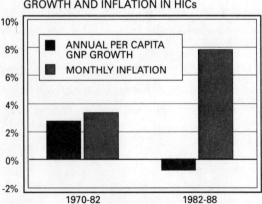

Figure 27
Since the Latin American debt crisis began in 1982, growth in heavily indebted countries has collapsed while inflation has soared.

During the years of the financing strategy, the obligations of countries were postponed in three ways. Repayment of principal was rescheduled; official agencies such as the IMF and the World Bank made new loans to the countries that could be used to pay part of the interest coming due; and the banks that had lent money to the countries in the first place were rounded up for so-called "concerted" lending, which amounted to indirect relending of part of the remaining interest. In effect, repayment of debt was very nearly halted, and limited new lending was arranged from both private and public sources.

This strategy could be, and was, described as a plan to put highly indebted countries still deeper into debt. In the early years of the debt problem, however, this did not seem like a bad idea. Given the rates of growth achieved by debtor nations in the past, and the economic reforms insisted on by the creditors as part of the package, it seemed likely that most of the major debtors could grow their way out of their debt problem. In other words, even though the debt might grow, the incomes of the debtors would grow faster—and thus the creditworthiness of the debtors would improve, not worsen, over time.

Unfortunately, things haven't worked out that way. The collapse of economic growth among debtors has discredited the idea that the debtor nations can grow out of their problem. Indeed, the ratio of debt to income has generally worsened over time.

As the failure of the financing strategy has become apparent, the secondary prices of Third World debt—the prices at which creditors are willing to sell their claims to others, a useful indicator of confidence—have plummeted.

Now the slow growth of debtors is not an accident. It has a lot to do with the debt itself—with the direct burden of debt service, and with the indirect effects on confidence and incentives of an over-

DEBT AS PERCENT OF GNP FOR HICs

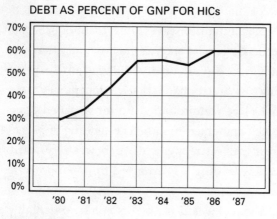

Figure 28
Highly indebted countries have not succeeded in growing their way out of debt; instead, the ratio of debt to their income has increased over time.

hang of debt that is larger than anyone expects the countries to pay. Thus there is a kind of vicious circle: Countries are failing to work their way out of the debt problem because of slow growth; and they are growing slowly at least in part because of their debt.

As recently as the beginning of 1989, the possibility of such a vicious circle was vigorously denied by U.S. officials and alluded to only guardedly by officials at the IMF and World Bank. The reason was obvious. If there is such a vicious circle, the debt must be reduced. Only since the Brady speech in early 1989 has it become respectable to call for partial debt forgiveness.

But how is such debt reduction to take place, and who is to pay for it? This is actually an easy question, but it is one that has not yet been squarely faced by U.S. policymakers.

Debt reduction

Let's ask the following question: How much would it cost *creditors* to forgive, say, $10 billion of Mexico's debt?

It certainly would not cost them $10 billion. Nobody has confidence that Mexico will pay all its debt; Mexican debt sells for only about 40 cents on the dollar on the secondary market. So the market value of the debt to be forgiven is really only $4 billion.

But even $4 billion is much too high an estimate. The secondary price reflects the fraction of the debt that creditors expect to be paid on average; the probability that Mexico will pay the last $10 billion is much less. Furthermore, reducing Mexico's debt would help its growth prospects, at least a little, and this would enhance the value of the remaining debt. So the value to the creditors of the last $10 billion in Mexican debt—the amount by which their expected payments would be reduced if they canceled that last $10 billion—is quite small.

It may even be negative. If the vicious circle of high debt and low growth is strong enough, reducing debt may actually enhance a country's prospects enough to increase the total expected debt repayment. Many economists working in this area have adopted the idea of a "debt Laffer curve," a curve that relates the market value of a country's debt to its nominal value.[12] At sufficiently high levels of debt the curve turns down, so reducing the obligations of a country increases its total expected payments. Some recent estimates suggest that for a number of smaller debtors, such as Peru and Costa Rica, debt reduction would actually benefit creditors as well as debtors. Larger debtors such as Argentina or Mexico may not be in this paradoxical position, but it is still true that the cost of debt reduction to the creditors is very small indeed.

---

12. I reluctantly report that the debt Laffer curve was first set out in a paper that I prepared for the IMF. The idea of a vicious circle of debt was expressed earlier in a less formal way by many people, notably Harvard's Jeffrey Sachs.

So we have concluded that reducing the debt of problem debtors would not cost their creditors very much; it would certainly cost them considerably less than the secondary market price of the debt, and it might even benefit them. But this leads to a fairly startling conclusion: *Large-scale debt relief would not cost very much.*

Here's the way the arithmetic works. The most heavily indebted countries owe about $400 billion. Suppose we wanted to carry out a massive debt relief scheme that cut the debt in half, to $200 billion. Suppose also that taxpayers in the creditor countries had to compensate banks for any losses that result from the scheme. This looks at first like so large a bailout that it would be politically unthinkable. But it isn't.

First, at current prices on the secondary market, the $400 billion face value of debt is worth only about $140 billion. So the market value of the debt to be canceled is only $70 billion.

Second, even this heavily overstates the amount by which private creditors would have to be compensated. The likelihood that the

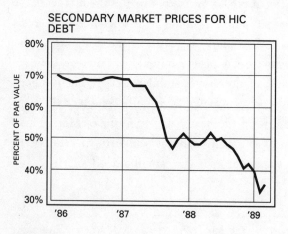

Figure 29
The secondary market prices of debt, a useful indicator of creditor confidence, have plummeted.

creditors would be paid in full is much less than the 35 percent secondary price on the average dollar of debt, and debt reduction would enhance the value of the debt remaining. So, overall, canceling $200 billion in claims would impose a cost on creditors of probably no more than $25 billion.[13]

Third, the United States is not the only major creditor nation. In fact, U.S. banks account for less than 40 percent of the bank lending to problem Third World debtors. In any big debt relief scheme, the U.S. share would be similar to its share of the original lending. So the total cost to U.S. taxpayers of massive Third World debt relief would be on the order of $10 billion.

As a one-time cost, rather than a continuing expense, this is a remarkably small number. For the sake of comparison, the savings and loan bailout has already been given $166 billion in funding, and most experts expect that sum to rise to $200 billion or more. *Massive debt relief for the Third World would cost U.S. taxpayers around one-twentieth of the expected cost of the S&L bailout.*[14]

13. A recent World Bank study concludes that the cost to creditors of one dollar of debt reduction for the typical highly indebted country is less than 10 cents.

14. Or if you prefer a tackier example, a massive debt bailout would cost about twice the sum stolen from the U.S. Department of Housing and Urban Development in the 1980s.

13   Corporate Finance

The August 1989 issue of *Fortune*, to the titillation of its readers, featured a story on the "CEO's second wife." On the cover was Carolyne Roehm, a glamorous former model and fashion designer. The article was revealing in many ways about the state of American society at the end of the 1980s, but one of the more unintentional lessons came in the choice of cover girl. For Roehm's husband is not a captain of industry in the traditional sense. He is Henry Kravis, driving force behind the investment firm of Kohlberg Kravis Roberts—a specialist in takeovers and leveraged buyouts. That is, Kravis has made his huge personal fortune not by building a productive enterprise in the usual sense, but by mediating in the rearrangement of existing firms' ownership.

This choice is no accident. The 1980s have been an era in which fabulous fortunes have been made in corporate finance. The heroes of the age have been the entrepreneurs, people like Apple's Steve Jobs or Lotus's Mitch Kapor. But the really big money has gone to the deal makers. If the late nineteenth century was the era of the robber barons, the 1980s were to an even greater extent that of the financial wizards. Indeed, the achievements of the sudden rich of the 1980s in many ways eclipsed those of the robber barons. The great nineteenth-century fortunes grew slowly, along with the enterprises they were tied to: mile by mile of railroad, steel mill by steel mill, refinery by refinery. The great fortunes of the 1980s came swiftly, sometimes in a matter of weeks, and often while their owners were still young enough to enjoy them to the fullest (hence the *Fortune* article).

The emergence of sudden wealth in the financial markets is one of the great spectacles of the age. We cannot understand our economy without understanding what it means. Specifically, we need to answer three questions. First, where is the wealth coming from? Second, why have a few individuals profited so massively? Third, why is this all happening now?

Where is the wealth coming from?

The financial operations that have created so much wealth for a few Americans require much more than a random reshuffling of paper. Indeed, they have involved two systematic changes in the structure of American industry. On one side, there has been a substantial shift in *control*, away from either the original owners or the original management. On the other, there has been a massive shift in *financing*, away from equity and toward debt.

What financial operators do is to facilitate the purchase of part or all of an existing company either by another company (a takeover) or by a group of investors that often includes the original management (a leveraged buyout, or LBO).[15] In either case the result is a shift of control. In a takeover the original management is displaced by the management of the acquiring firm. In an LBO the hired management stays, but the original board of directors is cut out.

---

15. In practice, many financial deals involve both LBO and takeover elements. For example, the group that buys a firm in an LBO may immediately sell off parts of the firm to other firms in order to pay off part of the debt they have just taken on.

Both takeovers and LBOs typically involve the creation of considerable amounts of corporate debt. The investors in an LBO do not usually have enough money to pay for the company out of their own pockets; they must borrow the money. The acquiring corporations in takeover battles also usually come up with the cash by borrowing. So both takeovers and LBOs lead to sharp increases in corporate debt. On the other side, the total quantity of corporate stock outstanding falls, as the stock is bought up by the acquiring firm or group of investors. The 1980s have been marked by a combination of large new issues of corporate debt together with a large *negative* net rate of issue of equity.

Both operations are also typically very expensive. Stock bought in either a takeover or an LBO typically sells for a premium of more than 50 percent over its previous market price. To this must be added substantial fees to the investment firms that arrange the deal. So a number of people make a lot of money. The original stockholders are paid substantially more than their stock was initially selling for. And the investment houses get enough to pay for a lot of expensive houses, parties, and, apparently, wives. The question is: Where does all this money come from?

Like so many issues in the past decade, this is a matter of bitter dispute among the experts. Within a five-minute walk from Cambridge's Harvard Square one can find the chief exponents of two radically opposed views.

The optimistic view is that of the Harvard Business School's Michael Jensen. According to Jensen, the rise in stock prices associated with the shift in control represents a gain in efficiency. That is, the new owners of a firm will simply manage the firm better than the people they replace. The market understands this, so when it sees that a takeover or LBO is imminent, it raises its estimation of what the stock is worth.

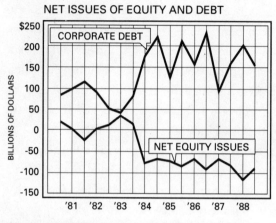

Figure 30
During the 1980s corporations have issued large amounts of debt, while re-
purchases of stock have greatly exceeded new issues.

A much more pessimistic view has been expounded by Jensen's
Harvard colleague Lawrence Summers—chief economic adviser to
the ill-fated Dukakis presidential campaign. Summers argues that
the gains come not from raising efficiency but by taking money
away from others. Summers and Andrei Shleifer of the University
of Chicago claim that the bulk of the rise in stock prices in takeovers
and LBOs comes from "breach of contract"—from breaking prom-
ises made by the original owners or management in return for past
favors. This is the Gordon Gekko image from the movie *Wall Street*:
Financial operators get rich by slashing wages, by firing workers
who had been promised job security, and by taking on a debt
burden that exposes existing holders of corporate debt to an unan-
ticipated risk of bankruptcy.

Which of these views makes the most sense? Let's look at them in
a bit more detail.

Efficiency gains

Michael Jensen has taken on the role of the chief academic defender of takeovers and LBOs. In his view, the gain to stockholders from corporate reshufflings is a gain to the economy; indeed, he likes to count up the increases in stock prices resulting from takeovers and LBOs and use the number as a measure of the contribution of investment houses to America's economic growth.

Where does Jensen think the gains come from? It's not that the acquiring managers are necessarily smarter than the people they replace. The potential for gain comes from the fact that managers traditionally have had too much independence. According to Jensen, in many corporations management has ceased to serve the interests of the shareholders. Top management hoards retained earnings to invest in projects that increase its power and perks instead of re-turning them to the stockholders; they invest in low-return but prestige-building ventures; they accept wasteful labor practices and poor management at lower levels rather than face unpleasant confrontations. How can they get away with this? Because stock-holders are too scattered and diverse a group to be fully informed about management's actions, or to act effectively if they are in-formed. Jensen argues that since the typical premium in a financial restructuring is 50 percent, the typical management was wasting about 30 percent of the stockholders' rightful returns.

Into this sloppy management setting come the new financial artists. They put control of the corporation into aggressive new hands—or, by making the managers the new owners, put new fire in their bellies. They also place the corporation under a debt burden that requires the managers to maximize profits simply to meet in-terest payments. The result? A new dedication to efficiency that makes millions for its engineers, but justifiably so, because it revi-talizes the firm.

What's wrong with this vision? While many people feel instinctively comfortable with the idea that the typical corporate management is lazy, self-aggrandizing, and generally unlikable, it is a little hard to believe that the observed stock premiums result solely from efficiency gains due to paper restructurings.

And surely the crucial question must be why, if corporate restructuring is so beneficial, the great wave of restructuring since 1980 hasn't had a more noticeable effect on America's economic growth. Hundreds of billions of dollars have been added to stock prices through such deals. Yet productivity growth remains hardly faster than in the 1970s, and America's economic and technological standing in the world continues its inexorable decline. If we're so rich, why aren't we smarter?

Jensen himself seems insensitive to some of the ironies involved in the divergence between stock prices and other measures of economic performance. In a paper presented to the 1988 "Predator's Ball" sponsored by Drexel Burnham Lambert (former home of junk bond king and accused insider trader Michael Milken), he provides a glowing portrait of the new, efficient corporate structures made possible by takeovers and LBOs. He then contrasts this happy modern situation with the bad old days when independent management, unaccountable to stockholders, felt free to squander corporate cash flow—a situation that, according to Jensen, "reached its peak in the mid to late 1960s." It does not seem to bother him that his bad times in the mid to late 1960s were an era of 3 percent annual productivity growth, rapidly rising living standards, and U.S. technological preeminence, while his modern era of efficiency is a time of 1 percent productivity growth, stagnant living standards, and relative decline.

No doubt Jensen is right that a takeover or LBO often produces a gain in economic efficiency. Both popular perception and the views of other experts suggest, however, that much if not most of the gains occur not from increasing wealth but from redistributing it.

Breach-of-contract

Lawrence Summers and Andrei Shleifer have taken on the role of "anti-Jensens," producing arguments against the corporate restructurings of the 1980s. Their case fits popular prejudice better than Jensen's. But let's see how it works.

Summers and Shleifer start with a scenario. Imagine a company that for some reason has long had a policy of paying its workers more than they could earn elsewhere. Suppose for the moment that this high-wage policy represents nothing more than weak management, which buys labor peace at stockholder expense. Following a corporate restructuring, a new lean, mean management changes this policy: It demands and gets wage cuts that raise profits and hence the value of the firm to stockholders.

What Summers and Shleifer point out is that in this case the rise in the stock price does *not* measure a gain to the U.S. economy as a whole. It simply reflects a redistribution of the existing pie, away from workers and to the stockholders. You may think this is a good thing or a bad thing, but either way it is wrong to follow Jensen's procedure and equate rises in stock prices with gains to the economy.

Summers and Shleifer claim that most of the added value from corporate restructuring results from a redistribution of income rather than an increase in efficiency. Wages are the most obvious target: In many firms workers are paid more than the minimum that would keep them from quitting, and the popular picture surely suggests that wage cuts are a common follow-up to LBOs and takeovers. Another target is the company's bondholders: By reducing its equity and taking on more debt, a restructured company can increase the upside potential for profits, while passing some of the downside risk to people who lent the company money in the past never imagining that the firm would put itself so deeply into debt. In 1988, when RJR Nabisco became the target of a leveraged buyout attempt (engineered by Kohlberg Kravis Roberts), the price of its outstanding bonds fell 16 percent.

At the very least, the Summers-Shleifer argument suggests that people like Jensen greatly overstate the gains from corporate restructuring, and that they are very wrong in arguing that almost everyone gains. But Summers and Shleifer go further, and suggest that the long-run effect may well be to make nearly everyone worse off.

Their argument is that most of the benefits taken away from workers and bondholders were not simple giveaways. Instead, they were part of long-term implicit understandings. Firms that pay above-market wages and protect job security do not necessarily do so because their managements are softhearted. They might also do it in exchange for long-term commitment and high morale on the part of their work force. Firms that keep their debt low are protecting their reputation so that they can continue to borrow at favorable rates. In effect, Summers and Shleifer argue, what happens following a corporate restructuring is the breaking of a set of unwritten contracts between a firm and its "stakeholders"—all of those other than its stockholders who have made a long-term commitment to the firm. Such unwritten contracts have no legal force; but then most business dealings are based on trust and on a concern for reputation, rather than on the letter of the law.

According to the breach-of-contract view, the corporate restructurings of the 1980s have produced a new disregard for the maintenance of long-term relationships. This leads to large immediate benefits for stockholders, as income is redistributed in their favor. But in the long run, it will mean that corporations find it harder to build up invisible assets like worker morale. The result will be slower economic growth and a lower standard of living for most Americans.

How does this thesis stand up against the facts? The claim that most of the gains of restructuring come from redistribution is more in harmony with what we know about the American economy in the past decade than the Jensen view. If Jensen were right, we should have seen a decade of great economic strides in productivity. We didn't. On the other hand, the Summers-Shleifer view would lead us to expect growing income inequality, with declining real wages for previously well-paid blue-collar workers in particular, as the counterpart of higher stock prices. And we have indeed seen all these things.

But their argument that the wage cuts sometimes associated with takeovers represent the breaking of an efficient long-term arrangement is more doubtful. They may be idealizing the past as much as Jensen idealizes the future. At a guess, when the target of a takeover paid premium wages, this was less because it represented an efficient long-term bargain than because sloppy management preferred not to bargain hard with workers.

A compromise view

There is certainly some truth to both the Jensen and Summers-Shleifer views of corporate restructuring. A compromise view might argue that the changing structure of the U.S. economy in the 1980s offered opportunities to raise the value of companies both by raising efficiency and by squeezing wages. Let's consider a story that may be helpful as a way of thinking about what happened.

According to this story, the corporate restructurings of the 1980s were largely motivated by the needs of economic restructuring—specifically, the need to dismantle "smokestack America."

In the 1960s and even during the 1970s, America's economic landscape was still dominated by the great corporations of the industrial heartland, and by the powerful unions that organized their workers. These blue-collar workers commanded wages well above what comparable workers earned elsewhere; but the firms they worked for, with long traditions of avoiding price competition, could easily pass these wage costs on to consumers.

Then came the trade deficit and the intensification of international competition. In the face of this competition it became necessary both to "downsize" smokestack America, withdrawing capital from traditional industrial sectors, and to cut the wages of industrial workers. These were tasks for which the existing management structure was ill suited. The managers of firms in the shrinking traditional industries were unwilling to return their cash flow to stockholders, even if there were higher-return investments available in other industries. Yet they lacked the knowledge to diversify profitably into new areas. They were also unwilling to confront their unions and seek givebacks and wage cuts.

Debt-financed takeovers and leveraged buyouts changed all that. Stockholders were bought out at a premium, and a large debt was incurred to finance the buyout. This debt both enabled and forced a change in management behavior. The burden of debt left managers little surplus cash flow to invest in the wrong place, and enforced a new toughness in labor negotiations. The restructured corporations had to be lean and mean to satisfy their creditors; and their new leanness and meanness retroactively justified the premium prices paid in the takeover.

This story contains elements of both Jensen and Summers. It agrees with Jensen that the value of corporate restructurings comes from the way they change management incentives, and that some of these gains represent a real gain to the economy, as capital is reallocated away from low-return sectors. But it also agrees with

Summers that many of the financial gains come not from increased efficiency but from cutting the incomes of previously well-paid workers. Moreover, it establishes a link between the financial fever of the 1980s and the rapid growth of inequality.

Why do some people make so much money?

Whichever Harvard professor is right about the ultimate reasons, the 1980s witnessed a record number of occasions in which a firm or a group of investors came to believe that a corporation was worth substantially more in their hands than in the hands of current management. So it is not surprising that there have been a large number of transactions in which corporations have changed hands.

What is a little more surprising is the exotic new world of financial practice that has rapidly emerged around the business of corporate restructuring. This new world includes previously unheard-of activities for firms, ranging from "greenmail" to "poison pills," from searches for "white knights" to "Pac-Man defenses." It has also created new professions, like risk arbitrage, which seem mysteriously lucrative, and turned previously obscure sins, like insider trading, into major sources of concern.

What's all this about? There is neither space nor need to describe all the details here—especially because this is a field in which some of the cleverest people in the country are engaged in developing new variations every day. But a few basic principles may help make sense of the wild new world of corporate finance.

The starting point is a seemingly simple insight on the economics of takeovers by economists Sanford Grossman of the Wharton School and MIT's Oliver Hart. Suppose, said Grossman and Hart in a now famous 1978 paper, that one firm has come to believe that by taking over another it can greatly enhance the target's value—say, that the acquired firm would be worth 50 percent more than the current value of its stock. Suppose also that it offers to buy the target from its stockholders. What price will those stockholders demand? More to the point, how much of the benefit of the takeover will accrue to the bought-out stockholders rather than to the acquiring firm?

The answer, according to Grossman and Hart, is that the stockholders will reap *all* of the benefits, that nothing will be left for the acquirer. As soon as stockholders know that the stock is worth 50 percent above its previous price to the acquirer, they will refuse to sell unless they get that price. So the market price will rise on the news of an impending takeover to a point that makes the takeover only barely worth carrying through.

But the cost of a takeover extends beyond the price of the stock. To prepare for a takeover requires research, time spent lining up financing, and much else. Unfortunately, these costs are already sunk by the time the bid is actually made, and, according to the Grossman-Hart analysis, the stockholders will not leave any margin in the price to help defray them. So according to their model, a takeover bid should always lose money, even if it really can raise the profitability of the target firm.

The Grossman-Hart analysis was intended, among other things, to explain why takeovers used to be relatively rare. In the 1980s, however, takeovers have become common. Why? At least part of the answer is that a shrewd acquirer can pick up a substantial part of the target company's stock *before* his intention to attempt a takeover becomes known. This initial stock purchase takes place at a lower price than the subsequent takeover bid, and so dilutes the transfer to the original stockholders. Of course, such a successful initial purchase must be surreptitious. If it becomes known that a potential acquirer is trying to buy a company's stock, the price will rise in anticipation.

Once one understands this need to buy as much of a target firm as possible on the sly, much of the wild world of corporate finance in the 1980s becomes comprehensible. First, the style of today's finance—half military exercise, half little boy's game—can be seen as a logical outgrowth of the dynamics of takeover, in which speed and surprise are essential, and in which getting information and deceiving rivals become the primary routes to success. Second, the new style of finance creates new professions. It has always been true that one could make a lot of money by figuring out what would happen to a company's stock in the near future. That used to require an assessment of the company's prospects. Today, however, the biggest cause of large changes in stock prices is the action of other companies. If you can figure out which companies will be targets of takeover or LBO attempts in the near future, you can achieve quick wealth. And so we have the emergence of risk arbitrage: the practice of buying up the stock of likely targets for restructuring.

How do risk arbitrageurs do their job? In principle, they can rely on careful assessment of the likely strategies of corporations, on movements in stock prices that suggest a takeover bid is in the works, on legally obtained intelligence about the movements and actions of key players. As anyone can see, however, there is another obvious and more certain way to know who is contemplating buying what: Pay someone who knows to tell you. Hence we have the rise of insider trading, the (eventual) fall of Ivan Boesky, and the trial of Michael Milken.

We know, then, how some people have gotten rich: The new world of corporate finance has both offered new levels of reward to investors who can outguess other investors and created the potential for a new kind of genteel crime. But the inevitably associated activities of risk arbitrage and insider trading need a few further comments.

First, risk arbitrage, even if done honestly, is one of the least productive activities ever devised. It is a sad commentary that some of the smartest, most energetic people in America make very comfortable livings trying to guess what some other smart people will be doing a few hours later. Matters are all the sadder, of course, if these best and brightest employ illegal methods to gain that extra edge.

On the other hand, it may be said that neither risk arbitrage nor even insider trading is inherently damaging to the economy. What does a risk arbitrageur do? He buys stock in the likely target of a takeover or LBO, and therefore makes the takeover more expensive. He is naturally more effective at this if he has inside information. The net effect is to discourage corporate restructurings. If corporate restructurings were always or even usually a good thing, this would be a cause for dismay. But as we have seen, there is a fairly good case against at least some restructurings. So a bit of sand in the wheels is not a great tragedy. It will be a while before Lawrence Summers starts singing the praises of Ivan Boesky, but in a perverse way they are allies.

The potential for abuse of trust built into the current world of corporate finance also helps explain why it pays so well—why freshly minted MBAs earn six-digit salaries, and why the princes of finance are paid sums almost beyond imagining. These are undoubtedly remarkable people, with steel nerves and quick judgment, operating in a business where tiny edges bring huge returns. But they are exposed to severe temptation. Bank managers are well paid, not only for their skills, but also because it is not always a good idea to entrust heavy responsibility to people paid a niggardly salary. Similarly, investment bankers are more reliable if they earn enough, and value their good name enough, to look temptation in the face and pass it by.

Why now?

Perhaps the most perplexing question about the spectacular re-structuring of corporate America in the 1980s is: Why now? Whether the money comes from efficiency gains (just wait and see), stealing the bread of honest workers and bondholders, or suckering gullible dentists who buy junk bonds, why this decade and not before?

Here are a few hypotheses:

First is the argument that Michael Milken produced the times, and not the other way around. Arguably (as Jensen, among others, does argue), the new corporate finance involves important innovations that make it possible for firms to carry more debt than before. (Notice, by the way, that even if this is true, it doesn't mean that buyouts are a good thing; these innovations could be financing breach of contract instead of increased efficiency.)

A second hypothesis is that changes in the political climate cleared the way for the new age. Many of the mergers of the past decade would have faced severe antitrust challenges in the 1970s; others would have brought once powerful unions into action, with tacit support from the Federal government. It is certainly a remark-able coincidence that so much new wealth emerged just as the body politic decided that it was OK to get rich. Maybe it wasn't a coinci-dence.

And there is one more possible explanation. To the extent that the whole enterprise has depended on downplaying the risk of junk bond finance, maybe the key was simply that enough time had passed since the last great financial crisis. Harvard's Benjamin Friedman has pointed out that while the risk of financial crisis is roughly constant over time, such crises occur so rarely that an estimate of their probability based only on recent experience will fluctuate between excessive pessimism (in the immediate aftermath of crisis) and totally unwarranted optimism (after a stretch of good luck). So maybe it was just the passage of time that laid the groundwork for the 1980s. Once the great buying spree had started, it became harder and harder for the pessimists to cling to their convictions—and off we went.

V   American Prospects

Americans no longer expect much from their economy or from the politicians who manage it. They appear to be satisfied so long as disaster is avoided and most people's living standards do not decline. And the most likely forecast for the 1990s is that Americans will get what they expect—no disaster, but no much good news, either.

Nonetheless, there are other possibilities. Anyone who confidently predicts what the next decade will be like is either foolish or dishonest, for if we learn anything from recent history it is how completely wrong expectations can be. In 1947 most economists were pessimists, expecting the return of mass unemployment. The extraordinary growth of the next 25 years surprised them all. In the early 1970s, by contrast, nearly everyone was excessively optimistic. None of the major economic difficulties of the 1970s and 1980s—the energy crisis, the productivity slowdown, the rise of European unemployment, the debt crisis—was foreseen. So history teaches us to be humble and to entertain a variety of possibilities.

This final part of the briefing book sketches out three scenarios: one in which everything works out just fine; one in which the irresponsible policies of the 1980s produce disaster in the 1990s; and finally a sort of central case in which we merely drift along, experiencing neither disaster nor striking success.

Two points should be emphasized about these scenarios. First, they represent an attempt to stay within the range of the plausible. Something wonderful or terrible could always happen—cold fusion could turn out to work, or the spread of AIDS could turn into a crippling burden. The scenarios presented here, however, are all based on relatively reasonable assumptions.

Second, these are scenarios, not forecasts. Looking back from the year 2010, we will surely marvel at our stupidity in 1990. We will wonder how we could have failed to notice those developments that would be crucial in the years ahead (spectacular economic growth in a liberalized Eastern Europe and Russia? a super savings and loan crisis as other hidden government liabilities come to light?). In short, these scenarios are illustrations of the kinds of things that might happen, not predictions of what will happen.

14   Happy Ending

The race is not to the swift, nor yet the battle to the strong, nor yet bread to the wise, nor yet flourishing economies to policymakers of understanding. It is perfectly possible that the American economy will, over the next decade, deliver a level of performance that will make our current anxieties look foolish and perhaps persuade our leaders that they were somehow responsible.

The key is productivity. If productivity growth in the United States were to recover to something like its rates of the 1950s and 1960s, practically everything would fall into place.

A productivity revival?

It's not too hard to make a case that productivity growth in the 1990s will be much better than it was in the 1970s or 1980s. In fact, there are at least four schools of productivity optimists: statistical, generational, managerial, and technological.

The statistical case for a productivity revival starts from the one sure fact in all of this: We don't know much about why productivity growth varies. In particular, we really don't know why productivity grew rapidly from 1945 to 1973, then very slowly thereafter. Since we don't know why growth slowed, we cannot confidently argue that it might not speed up again.

The history of U.S. productivity growth in the twentieth century can be read as encouraging. Looking back at the 10-year average rates of productivity growth shown in Figure 6, we see that this rate has fluctuated around 2 percent, sometimes more, sometimes less. Never mind why: Suppose that it turns out that the 1950s and 1960s were just a lucky draw, and the 1970s and 1980s a bad one. There is no reason that the 1990s shouldn't be another good draw, with productivity growth above 2 percent—and perhaps as high as 3 percent. Judging from the figure, that's well within the range of the possible.

The technological argument for a productivity revival occurs to almost anyone who reads the "science and technology" section of his favorite business magazine. Technologically, the past 15 years have been a parade of wonders: Especially in computation, but also in communication (remember life before the fax?), there has been one revolution after another, with new areas such as biotechnology now seemingly on the verge of widespread practical implementation. Yet economically, the news has been generally dreary—a typical American worker can buy less with his pay today than his father could when Richard Nixon was first inaugurated.

Something is out of kilter here. Either technology isn't all it's cracked up to be, or we haven't yet seen the impact of the new technology on our economy. Maybe the next decade will see businesses learn how to use computers, faxes, and fiberoptics to do something really useful, and the rate of growth will pick up. The highest rate of U.S. productivity growth before the 1950s was in the 1920s, driven by the automobile industry—even though automobiles had been in existence and even in fairly widespread use since the turn of the century. We are arguably in the same situation with regard to personal computers: They are around, but only now are we about to use them creatively to transform our lives.

The managerial argument for rapid growth is something that we already encountered in the discussion of corporate finance. Suppose that Michael Jensen is largely right, and that most of the gains from takeovers and buyouts reflect increases in economic efficiency as lax management is either replaced or given incentives to serve investor interests. And suppose that it is really true that people such as Michael Milken have developed an organizational form for the modern firm that will allow productive restructuring throughout the economy. Then the takeover-buyout boom of the 1980s may turn out to be the prologue to a period of rapid productivity growth.

Lastly, the generational argument for accelerating growth simply points out that the 1960s are receding into the past. If you think that the ultimate source of the productivity problem lies in the fact that too many talented people dropped out, wasted years trying to become social workers, and/or avoided entrepreneurial or corporate careers because of misplaced idealism, then you would expect to see faster growth as the success-oriented post–baby-boom generation makes its way into the work force.

None of these arguments is conclusive. Indeed, it is easy enough to offer a counterargument to each one. My own view is much more pessimistic—I worry about the poor quality of U.S. education, about the growth of the underclass, about the short-term bias of investment, about government neglect of infrastructure, and I worry that productivity growth may actually decline. The truth, however, is that nobody knows.

The consequences of a productivity boom

Suppose that the optimists turn out to be right, and that U.S. productivity grows much faster in the decade ahead than it did in the past 15 years—say, at close to 3 percent a year. How would this affect the economy?

The answer is that it would make many, but not all, of the problems discussed in this book fade away.

To begin with, rapid productivity growth would lead to a general rise in living standards. If productivity were to grow as fast in the 1990s as it did in the 1960s, the average American worker's take-home pay would grow by something like 30 percent. Unless there were an extraordinary further increase in inequality, this growth in income would be widely shared. As a result, the era of growing misery at the bottom of the income scale would be over.

Faster productivity growth would also do a great deal to defuse the problem of the trade deficit through a variety of indirect channels. First, faster growth would raise tax revenues. While some demands on the public purse would also grow more rapidly (like demands for increased infrastructure investment), others—notably defense and interest on the public debt—would not. So the budget deficit would fade away, and as a consequence the national savings rate would rise, contributing to a decline in the trade deficit.

At the same time, faster growth would minimize the consequences of trade deficits. While claims of foreigners on the U.S. economy would continue to rise (at least for a while), they would be a smaller piece of a larger pie and would thus create less of a drain. And a U.S. economy that was doing relatively well would probably experience less conflict with Japan, even if Japan were doing still better.

Faster productivity growth would not, of course, solve every economic problem, and it may be useful to remind ourselves of what it would not do. It would not necessarily reduce the unemployment rate: America did very well at containing unemployment during the 1970s and 1980s, despite low productivity growth, while Europe did badly, despite substantially faster productivity growth. It would not necessarily help reduce inflation: Inflation in the U.S.

first took off in the high-growth 1960s and was brought largely under control in the low-growth 1980s. It would not even protect the economy form the risks of financial crisis: Both the 1929 crash and the 1982 Latin American debt crisis followed decades of unusually high productivity growth in their victims.

Still, it is important to realize that a spontaneous productivity revival that would not be out of line with past experience could solve most of the pressing economic issues facing the United States without any positive action from our leadership. We could simply get lucky. On a purely unscientific basis, I would assign this kind of happy ending a probability of 20 percent.

15   Hard Landing

Despite the general contentment of the American public with their country's economic performance, predictions of catastrophe—doomsday books—still do a brisk business. While most of these predictions (the ones that sell best) are pure fantasy, there is a widespread undercurrent of concern that somehow the excesses of the 1980s—the budget deficit, the trade deficit, the growth of corporate debt—have prepared the ground for a future crisis.

Where might such a crisis come from? Popular books on economic crisis usually draw their images from 1929: a collapse of business confidence leading to global financial collapse. But a 1929-style crisis is quite unlikely in the modern world, for reasons to be discussed in a moment. A better bet is a crisis arising from the U.S. trade deficit and growing foreign debt—a crisis on Latin American lines.

1929 again?

The image of 1929 still haunts many Americans: the bubble of optimism suddenly bursts, stockbrokers leap from windows, prosperity vanishes almost overnight. Can it happen again?

It depends on what you mean. Can a stockmarket crash like that of 1929 happen again? Yes, of course it can—in fact, it already has. The initial fall in U.S. stock prices in the 1987 crash was as large as that of 1929, and the collapse spread around the world faster and more thoroughly. Could such a crash generate another depression? No. It didn't in 1987, and it almost surely won't the next time it happens.

By purely financial measures, the crash of 1987 was every bit as bad as the initial financial panic in 1929. The initial fall in the U.S. stock prices was slightly larger in 1929; but in 1987 the U.S. fall was much more nearly matched by the decline abroad. So on a global basis Black Monday in 1987 was actually worse than Black Thursday in 1929.

But from that point on the stories diverge totally. The initial crash in 1929 was followed by a deepening recession and by successive waves of further stock decline. The 1987 crash was followed by relatively rapid economic growth and a corresponding recovery of stock prices that soon erased virtually all of the initial drop.

Why didn't 1987 play like 1929? The basic answer is a surprising one, given today's widespread cynicism about economic policy and the role of government: We've learned something since 1929, and the Federal Reserve used that knowledge effectively. Stock market crashes need not cause severe downturns in the real economy. The crash in 1929 helped intensify a recession that was already developing. Even a year later that recession seemed unpleasant, but not menacing. What really turned the crash into the Depression was the collapse of the banking system in 1931, which led to a huge contraction in the availability of credit. In the judgment of most of those who have studied the events, this banking collapse was simply unnecessary. It happened only because of the almost eerie passivity of the Federal Reserve, which failed to do anything to stop it, permitting massive deflation and monetary collapse in the early 1930s.

In 1987 the Federal Reserve chose not to repeat its previous mistake. Faced with the stock crash, it rapidly expanded the supply of base money. The rest is already history. Instead of a depression, there was faster growth in the year following the crash than in the year before. Indeed, the 1987 crash may actually have improved the economy's performance by leading to a rise in the personal savings rate. The Fed demonstrated that it is not only possible but fairly easy to insulate the real economy from a financial panic.

Of course a misguided or incompetent Federal Reserve could still manage to turn some future stock crash into something serious. On a true gold standard, for example, or with a rigid monetarist rule in effect, the Federal Reserve would have been unable to carry out the rapid credit expansion of late 1987. Given reasonably competent and flexible management, however, there does not seem to be any reason to expect a repeat of 1929.

A U.S. debt crisis?

It is the spring of 1992, and the deterioration of the U.S. trade position predicted by many economists has proceeded faster than expected: First-quarter numbers indicate a trade deficit running at an annual rate of more than $200 billion. At the same time, inflation has gradually accelerated to about a 6 percent annual rate, and the Federal Reserve has tightened its policy in an effort to rein in the price rise, leading to a mild recession that has raised unemployment to 6.4 percent. The combination of a widening trade gap and the recession lead to widespread layoffs of manufacturing workers.

The trade gap also contributes to a growing mood of economic nationalism, fed both by trade and by the never-ending stream of conspicuous sales of U.S. real estate and firms to foreign nationals. The Democrats have discovered that the Japan issue is a Republican weak point: The Republican party was slow to realize that trade conflict had replaced the Cold War as the focus of public anxiety over foreign policy. The large sums accepted from Japanese sources by former high government officials, while generally legal, add to the bad taste left by the 1991 influence-buying scandal. Pollsters tell the Democratic leadership that the Japan issue can win the election for them, and tell the Republicans that they must act extra tough on Japan to counteract a public perception that they are soft on foreign economic interests.

In this highly flammable situation, the spark comes from the auto industry. Large-scale entry into the U.S. market by Japanese firms, who in 1991 produce almost 3.5 million cars and trucks in the United States, has led to substantial overcapacity; this overcapacity becomes severe when the recession and rising imports cut into domestic shipments. When General Motors announces a number of plant closings, blaming competition from Japanese firms producing here, there are widespread calls for limits on foreign ownership. When one of the major Japanese manufacturers itself announces that it is closing one of its U.S. plants, however, there is an overwhelming demand for restrictions not only on the ability of foreign firms to invest in the United States but also on their freedom to pull their money out.

Analysts later agree that it was the combination of fears of confiscatory U.S. policies toward foreign investment and worries about the U.S. trade deficit that started wholesale capital flight in the late spring. The dollar quickly drops to 95 yen. There it is briefly stabilized by a combination of large Treasury purchases of dollars on the foreign exchange market, financed by short-term loans from the governments of Germany and Japan, and 15 percent interest rates that attract some short-term private funds. But attempts to regain the confidence of foreign long-term investors are unsuccessful, not least because the few major acquisitions of U.S. firms that take place are widely denounced as "fire sales" due to the weak dollar.

At this point, there is a crucial policy error. As a severe recession looms on the verge of an election, the Federal Reserve loses its nerve and temporarily loosens policy. This move proves disastrous: The dollar drops to 60 yen, and inflation, thanks in part to the global oil crisis, accelerates within a year to more than 20 percent. The subsequent IMF-supervised stabilization program drives unemployment to 13 percent in 1994, and U.S. industrial output does not regain its 1991 level until 1997. . .

This is a fairly lurid fantasy—but not wildly unreasonable. The United States has a current account deficit of almost 2.5 percent of GNP right now, and this gap may widen to more than 3 percent over the next few years. A loss of confidence by international investors could easily force the United States to move into a current account surplus, potentially requiring a reduction in U.S. domestic demand relative to output of as much as 4 to 5 percent. The associated fall in the dollar would reduce U.S. real income by several additional percentage points. Put it all together and it becomes plausible that we could face a shock more severe than either the 1973 or the 1979 oil shocks. Each of those shocks sent inflation into double digits; the 1979 shock also sent unemployment above 10 percent and precipitated the massive recession of the early 1980s.

In 1985 Stephen Marris of the Institute for International Economics laid out a scenario for a "hard landing" based on a collapse of investor confidence in the dollar. When the dollar began sliding, right on schedule, Marris's prophecy seemed to be coming true. But the dollar slide did both much less harm and much less good than Marris had imagined: The trade deficit remained stubbornly high, but the inflationary impact was also mild. As the dollar stabilized in 1987, and eventually began to strengthen again, the hard landing scenario began to lose followers. A growing body of opinion claims that a hard landing of the sort Marris described cannot happen.

The optimism that has now become conventional wisdom has two components: a belief that the United States will continue to receive foreign financing for as long as it needs it; and a belief that even if foreigners do become reluctant to invest in the United States, leading to a decline of the dollar, no serious adverse effects will result. This conventional wisdom is probably right. But the truth is that we don't really know; just because Marris's hard landing hasn't happened yet doesn't mean that it can't happen.

Prospects for foreign financing

The United States is the world's largest debtor and continues to sell assets to foreigners at a near-record pace. Why should anyone think that this can go on almost indefinitely?

There are at least four reasons now being widely advanced to justify the belief that we can continue to finance massive current account deficits for many years to come. One of these reasons is a good point. The other three are just wrong.

The good point is that while U.S. foreign debt and its current account deficit are huge, so is the U.S. economy—and the dollar value of U.S. output increases over time due to both real growth and inflation. As a result, even deficits and debts that sound inconceivably large may not be overwhelming burdens. Suppose, for example, that the United States continues to run current account deficits at the rate of $120 billion every year from now until the end of the century, so that by the year 2000 our net foreign investment position is a negative $2 trillion. This sounds like an impossible sum. Yet if growth and inflation continue at recent rates, this would be less than 20 percent of GNP, and the net investment income of foreigners in the United States would be well within our ability to pay.

Matters will, of course, look different if the current account deficit widens instead of stabilizing; but it remains true that when the deficit is expressed as a share of national income instead of as a raw number, the instinctive reaction that the United States is on a wildly unsustainable course becomes hard to justify.

So much for the good reason not to worry about continued financing. What about the bad reasons?

One widely expressed view is that America will not have any financing problems because, even with rapid growth in U.S. foreign debt, claims on America will remain a small part of the portfolios of international investors. This is the argument offered in a recent report by the Bank for International Settlements (BIS), which concludes that since the share of claims on the United States in international portfolios will remain modest, "the financing of further large deficits on the current account of the U.S. balance of payments through inflows of foreign private capital need not lead to major financial market disturbances in the coming years."

Unfortunately, while it is true that claims on the United States will not be an overwhelming share of world portfolios in the next five or even ten years, it is also irrelevant. After all, claims on Mexico and Brazil never became large parts of world portfolios either; that didn't prevent a Latin American debt crisis. The point is that it is not the ratio of claims on the United States to the rest of the world's assets that matters—it is the ratio of those claims to the expected ability and/or willingness of the United States to pay.

A second bad argument is that the United States has a special position because of the international role of the dollar. In much of the world, the dollar serves as a unit of account: Much international trade is invoiced in dollars, much international lending and borrowing is denominated in dollars, and much international liquidity takes the form of dollar accounts. The argument is that this somehow means that the rest of the world automatically finances our deficits.

There are two things wrong with this view. First, it takes the special role of the dollar for granted. But in fact the outlines of emerging European and Japanese currency blocs can already be seen; this will surely cut into the dollar's special role. More important, the fact that the U.S. dollar is widely used as a unit of account does not mean that people around the world are obliged to accept dollar bills that the United States prints, or to put money into the U.S. economy. If a Japanese bank makes a loan to Turkey, payable in U.S. dollars, the use of the dollar is simply a convenience. Nobody has to put money in the United States. Dollar bank accounts do not necessarily have much to do with the United States. You can get a Eurodollar account in London, and if you withdraw your money, you get dollars. But, like any bank, the bank in London will carry only a limited reserve of dollars, investing most of its deposits wherever it sees the highest return. Even a bank account in the United States need not help finance the U.S. current account deficit, except to the limited extent that reserves have to be held. Money deposited in a bank in New York is just as likely to be lent abroad as money placed in banks in London or Singapore.

Suppose that investors around the world begin to doubt whether the United States will remain willing to service its foreign debt, or to allow foreign firms in the United States to send as much of their profits home as they like. Will the fact that the dollar is an international currency somehow prevent capital flight from the United States? Of course not.

The most recent argument for not worrying about the dollar is the growing tendency of foreigners to invest in the United States by buying real estate and firms, rather than debt. To many observers this seems to eliminate worries about debt service. To quote the BIS study again, "foreign direct investment . . . does not constitute external debt the servicing of which represents a fixed charge." But foreign firms are not investing here for their health. A dollar invested in the United States will eventually generate profits that accrue to those foreign owners. Since direct investment typically yields a higher rate of return than simple lending, the eventual cost to U.S. residents of a dollar invested directly will be larger than the cost of a dollar borrowed. If we think that the eventual constraint on U.S. foreign debt will be doubts about our willingness rather than our ability to repay them, it is worth bearing in mind that foreign-owned real estate and factories are even better targets for economic nationalism than foreign-owned bonds.

In sum, there is really only one valid argument in support of the belief that the United States can go on running current account deficits: the argument that a huge and growing U.S. economy can take on a massive debt load without really becoming overburdened.

But there is a reason not to feel entirely comfortable with this argument, either: the experience of the Latin American nations. During the 1970s, and right up to the edge of the crisis, the general verdict of economists was that the growth of Latin debt did not represent a problem, because part of the real value of the debt was eroded by inflation and the rest of the borrowing was being used to finance growth. In April 1981, to take a representative example, Harvard economist Jeffrey Sachs wrote that "much of the growth in LDC debt reflects increased investment and should not pose a problem of repayment . . . This is particularly true of Brazil and Mexico." Only 16 months later Mexico announced that it was stopping payments on its debt; Sachs himself has become the leading advocate of large-scale cancellation of Third World debt.

Nor was it only economists who failed to perceive the seriousness of debt growth in Latin America; virtually no one foresaw the problem. In the survey of country risk analysts published by

Institutional Investor in April 1982—only four months before the Mexican payment stoppage—the Latin debtors received reasonably good grades, with Mexico actually rated above South Korea.

As a matter of pure economics, the United States could continue to run deficits at the current rate for the next ten years without putting itself into an unsustainable position—and there is a good chance that it will get away with doing just that. But as foreign ownership of U.S. assets continues to grow, economic nationalism in the United States will increase. This will make foreigners justifiably nervous about the security of their investments. If this nationalism gets out of hand—or even if foreigners *think* that it might get out of hand—there will be capital flight from the United States that could quickly spiral, Latin American–style, into a full-fledged balance of payment crisis. The further the United States gets into debt, the larger this risk becomes. So a cutoff of foreign financing sometime during the 1990s remains a real possibility.

But this is only half of the hard-landing story. The scenario calls not only for capital flight and a plunging dollar but for disastrous macroeconomic effects as well. Are these likely?

Macroeconomics of crisis

If foreigners lose confidence in the United States, the immediate impact will be a fall in the dollar. But so what? From early 1985 to early 1987 the dollar lost roughly half its value in terms of the yen and the mark. Yet this slow-motion financial crash did no more damage than the fast-forward fall in stock prices that followed. Unemployment continued to decline; inflation accelerated only slightly. If stock market panics don't have to cause recessions, isn't the same true of foreign exchange market panics?

Not necessarily. When the stock market crashes, an active Federal Reserve can turn the crash into a purely paper event with no real consequences. If foreigners lose confidence in the United States, by contrast, there is an unavoidable real adjustment: We have to start spending no more than we earn. Nothing the Federal Reserve can do will force foreigners to continue to finance the U.S. current account deficit if they are unwilling to do so.

Can this real adjustment be made smoothly? The experience of the 1970s and 1980s is not encouraging. The 1982 debt crisis in Latin America derailed growth in that region for the rest of the decade. The oil crises of 1973 and 1979 represented shocks similar to a hypothetical hard landing for the dollar; they produced sharp inflationary spikes and deep recessions both at home and abroad. The only encouraging experience is that of the decline of the dollar from 1985 to 1987. And there are several reasons for doubting that this experience will be repeated.

First, what happened from 1985 to 1987 was not a full-fledged cutoff of capital inflows to the United States. Instead, as the dollar declined investors eventually became convinced that U.S. assets were cheap at current prices, and the dollar stabilized without having to fall enough to balance U.S. trade. In fact, the U.S. current account deficit, and hence the need for foreign financing, continued to grow for two years after the dollar started falling, due to lagged effects of the dollar's previous rise. Even in 1989 foreign capital inflows were about 2.5 percent of GNP, compared with 3.4 percent in 1986. Contrast this with Mexico, where a cutoff of foreign lending forced the country to move from a trade deficit of 2 percent of GNP in 1981 to a trade surplus of 5 percent in 1984, and we see that the United States has not yet known what it means to face the music.

Second, the fact that the decline of the dollar came immediately after an equally rapid rise dampened the effect on U.S. inflation. The strong dollar had not, by early 1985, been fully reflected in import prices. When the dollar rose, many foreign firms didn't cut their dollar prices, they simply increased their profit margins. As a result, when the dollar fell they could absorb a substantial part of that fall by cutting into their profit margins. Japanese firms in particular absorbed about half of the yen's rise by cutting their export prices relative to the prices they charged domestic customers. This response may have frustrated U.S. firms hoping that the lower dollar would help them win back markets, but it helped prevent any inflationary surge in the United States.

Also helping to hold down inflation was good luck on world raw material markets. The price of oil crashed in 1985, just as the dollar fell, offsetting inflationary pressures; other raw material prices fell to new lows in real terms. In 1978 and 1979 a falling dollar interacted with soaring raw material prices to produce an inflationary surge. In the years since 1985 the U.S. economy has had much better luck.

Lastly, the fall of the dollar took place at a time when the U.S. economy was operating with some slack capacity and with declining inflationary expectations. That meant that any pain from reduced foreign funding could be more than offset by increased output, as the Federal Reserve allowed the unemployment rate to fall from 7 to 5.3 percent.

If you want to envision a real hard landing, simply imagine that each of these factors is reversed. Suppose that foreigners face a perceived risk that is not alleviated by a lower dollar—such as fears of expropriation. Suppose that the resulting dollar crash follows a period of dollar stability, so there is no cushion to brake the rise in import prices, and that we have the bad luck (or lack of foresight) to stumble into a third oil crisis just as the dollar plunges. And suppose that the U.S. economy is already having an inflation problem when the crisis hits. What you get is a recipe for a truly disastrous hard landing.

This hard-landing scenario could happen, but it doesn't have to, even if policy continues to drift. Foreigners probably will continue to finance our deficits; even if they don't, we might handle the situation well enough to avoid a crisis. I give the hard landing a 25 percent chance of happening.

16   Drift

This final scenario is the one that comes closest to a forecast. It describes a U.S. economy in which tomorrow is much like today: in which there are no radical developments, either favorable or unfavorable, that make the economy of the 1990s very different from that of the late 1980s. In this scenario economic policy continues much as it has, with no major departures.

There are some countries for which this kind of scenario would be patently absurd. In a country like Peru, to take an extreme example, one can look at the evaporating foreign exchange reserves and declare that either a massive change in policies or a slide into anarchy must occur within a few months. The United States is not in that kind of situation. There is nothing in the basic arithmetic of U.S. budget deficits, foreign debt, or inflation that would prevent us from continuing more or less with current policies for another decade.

So let us suppose that the United States manages to drift along with no radical departures. What might the economy look like?

The domestic economy

The most likely forecast for the U.S. domestic economy in the 1990s is that it will look a lot like 1988–1989: fairly slow growth, modestly rising incomes for most Americans, generally good employment performance, a gradual acceleration of inflation.

If U.S. productivity growth does not accelerate, U.S. economic growth will actually have to slow down a little in the 1990s. The reason is demographic: The baby boomers are all now in the work force, and the great increase in female participation will probably not continue at the same rate. So in this central scenario we would see the U.S. economy grow at an average of slightly more than 2 percent a year over the next decade.

Median family income, however, probably would do little better than in the 1980s, partly because the number of families will not grow as fast, and partly because we would not expect the rising income of the most affluent to siphon off as much of the total growth in income as it did in the Reagan years. So the average family might gain about 10 percent in real income over the course of the decade. Assuming that the widening of the gap between highly skilled and less skilled workers will not continue, the 1990s will also differ from the 1980s in showing some rise in income for many of the poor. At the very bottom, however, everything we know points to a growing and ever more miserable underclass; the number of truly desperate poor will grow, as will the associated social pathologies. In other words, the middle class will probably do better in the 1990s than in the 1980s, but the ugly contrast between great affluence for one minority and intense poverty for another should be even greater in the year 2000.

Meanwhile, unemployment probably will drift down. As the labor force gets older and more experienced, the NAIRU will be lower. By the end of the decade, the unemployment rate could be between 4 and 5 percent.

As for inflation, it seems clear that the country does not want to pay the price of a serious drive to reduce the inflation rate. And if the continual pressure on the Federal Reserve to avoid even a slight recession is any guide, our leaders appear prepared to take more risks on the side of inflation than on the side of recession. The rule seems to be that when the Fed thinks there might be a recession, but isn't sure, it is under pressure to loosen policy just in case; when it thinks that inflation may be picking up, but isn't sure, it is expected to wait and see before tightening. This implies a persistent bias toward higher inflation. It would not be surprising if inflation has crept up to 7 percent by the end of the decade. Given what we have said about the costs of inflation, however, this will do almost no real harm.

The international economy

If the domestic U.S. economy in the year 2000 may look fairly similar to its current state, the international economy—and the role of the United States in that international economy—will almost surely look quite different.

In the first place, foreigners will own quite a lot of America. Net foreign claims on the United States will be something like 20 percent of GNP, with interest and dividends on these claims nearly 2 percent of national income. More strikingly, foreign-owned corporations will play a big role in the U.S. economy. It would not be surprising if, by the year 2000, foreign firms account for 25 percent of U.S. manufacturing production and own 45 percent of our banking sector.

This widespread foreign ownership will be a blow to traditional views of America's place in the world, a blow reinforced by the realities of international economic influence. By the year 2000, an increasingly unified Europe will have a larger GNP than America's, and Japan will have a GNP that in dollar terms is 80 percent or more of the U.S. level. Both Europe and Japan will have substantially larger exports than the United States, and both will have larger overseas investment—Japan in particular. So by many measures the United States will have sunk to the number three economic power in the world. We will still be the leading military power, but if the Soviet empire continues to dissolve at the current rate, this will be almost irrelevant.

The risk of nationalistic U.S. reaction in these circumstances— Gary Shilling's shift from Star Wars to Trade Wars— is obvious. If we fail to rise above our instincts, and if the Europeans and the Japanese follow suit, the 1990s will see a steady growth of trade restrictions. There may be no open rupture of the existing trade treaties, but they will be bypassed in various ways. The world will therefore tend to break apart into three trading blocs: North American, European, and East Asian. In this, at least, the near future will be different from the recent past: The effects of trade restrictions should be enough to reverse the trend of growing international economic integration. At least as far as trade goes, the world economy is likely to be *less* unified in the year 2000 than it is today.

Can this happen? Don't modern technologies of transportation and communication imply an ever more integrated world economy, whatever governments may do? History tells us otherwise. Economic nationalism can easily reverse the long-term trend toward a more integrated world economy for decades at a time.

Consider what happened to world trade for much of the twentieth century. We tend to assume that world economy is something that needs widebody jets and fax machines. But the truth is that these technologies are minor improvements from an economic point of view. The really decisive technologies for creating an integrated world economy were steamships, railroads, and telegraphs. These made the costs of shipping goods and transferring information low. Everything since has only further reduced costs that were already low by 1880. By 1913 our great-grandfathers had created an international economy that in many respects—mobility of labor, mobility of long-term capital—was more closely integrated than anything the world has seen since. Figure 31 shows a useful

SHARE OF TRADE IN NATIONAL INCOME

Figure 31
The long-term trend toward international integration can be reversed for decades
at a time by economic nationalism. Trade was a larger share of both American
and British national income before World War I than it was again until the 1970s.

measure, the ratio of total trade (exports plus imports) to GNP, for
Britain and the United States for selected dates since the mid-
nineteenth century. The figure reveals that large-scale trade is
nothing new; the United Kingdom was more of a trading nation in
the reign of Queen Victoria than the United States ever has been or
probably ever will be.

The figure also reveals something else: the extraordinary decline
in international trade after 1913. There is no mystery about what
happened in between: Nationalism and the resulting increase in
protectionism depressed trade to much lower levels than technology made possible.

Something similar, although milder, is likely in the years ahead.
World trade outside the trading blocs will grow more slowly than
world output, and might even shrink in real terms.

This is an unfortunate prospect, but not a terrible one. As pointed
out previously, the costs of protectionism are often exaggerated.

The kind of fragmentation of global markets envisioned here could reduce world output by 1 percent or possibly even 2 percent from what it otherwise would have been by the end of the century. That is an enormous cost in absolute terms—say, $250 billion a year at current prices—but it would not have a severe negative impact on living standards.

There is one major tension in this scenario. Suppose that economic nationalism leads to a slowing of growth in world trade. If the United States is to finance its continuing trade deficits, it must continue to attract foreign investment. Yet if current trends persist, foreign ownership will soon be a very conspicuous factor in our economy. What if the same economic nationalism that leads to trade restrictions also scares off foreign investors? Then we go back to our hard-landing scenario.

Barring such a crisis, however, the U.S. economy can live with an increasingly protectionist world; it can even deliver modest increases in living standards to its population.

Looking back at the future

To many Americans this scenario will sound reasonably good. There is no crisis; most people are better off. If the economy actually delivers fairly steady growth at more than 2 percent for the next decade, if inflation remains in single digits, if unemployment stays at roughly current levels, most people will count the decade a success. There will doubtless be caustic remarks from politicians and journalists about the foolishness of those doomsayers who claimed that the trade and budget deficits would bring catastrophe.

Yet this is a scenario that falls far short of what used to be regarded as successful performance. Twenty years ago, it was taken for granted that the rapid productivity growth of the postwar period, and the corresponding growth in living standards, would continue. When Herman Kahn and associates examined the prospects for the U.S. economy in their 1967 book *The Year 2000*, their most pessimistic scenario called for 2.5 percent annual productivity growth—and they argued strongly that at least 4 percent was more likely. That same year, in another series of essays on the year 2000, *Fortune* magazine projected that real wages by then would climb by 150 percent.

Imagine confronting these forecasters with a nation where productivity increased little more than 1 percent a year, where real hourly wages fell through the 1970s and 1980s, where poverty grew in absolute terms. They would have regarded such an outcome as a highly implausible disaster. They would also have predicted a drastic political reaction—especially if one added to the story greatly increased wealth at the top of the income distribution, a declining American position in the world, and growing foreign ownership of U.S. assets.

Yet this scenario now looks perfectly acceptable, and might even be regarded as a success. What is truly remarkable about our times is that the political system accepts our reduced prospects with so much equanimity.

In his 1971 novel *Love in the Ruins*, Walker Percy succinctly described the view of the future as it looked in the politically apocalyptic but economically sunny 1960s: "The center did not hold. However, the gross national product continues to rise." He got it exactly wrong. The GNP didn't continue to rise—at least not as fast as we thought it would. But things didn't fall apart, and the center held after all. And given the diminished expectations Americans now have for their economy, that is probably the way it will be for the next decade.

Index

Pages in italics indicate illustrations.

Airport economics, *x*
American Economic Association, 69
American Enterprise Institute, 129

Baker, James (Treasury Sec.), 89
Bank of England, crisis in, 87
Bank for International Settlements (BIS),
  183
Barro, Robert, 72
Base money
  and Federal Reserve, 79–80
  and multiplier effect, 80
Bhagwati, Jagdish, 129–130
Bilateral trade, U.S., *120*
Boesky, Ivan, 165
Bonfire of the Vanities (Wolfe), 19
Borrowing, real cost of, 53n1
Boskin, Michael, 76
Bradley, Sen. Bill, 82
Brady, Nicholas (Treasury Sec.)
  and debt reduction strategy, 146
Brander, James, 109n8
Breach of contract, 156, 159–161
Britain, total trade vs. GNP, *195*
Brookings Institution, 119n11
Budget deficit, 63–78
  and cutting domestic demand, 49–50
  and national savings, 68–69
  reducing, 74–77
  and trade deficits, 42–43
  view from left, 69–71
  view from right, 72–73
Burns, Arthur, 81
Bush, Pres. George
  and economic contentment, 1
  economic team of, 16
  on price stability, 59
Buy-Japanese policy, 127

Capital flight, potential for, 186
Capital flows, and trade, 44
Carter, Pres. Jimmy
  appoints Volcker, 58
  inflation and, 54
Cline, William, on dollar depreciation,
  98
Comparative advantage, 106
Competitiveness, loss of U.S., 47
Concerted lending, 147
Corporate debt
  increases in, 155
  and inflation, 53
  and net equity issues, *156*
Corporate finance, potential for abuse of
  trust in, 166
Corporate restructuring
  as beneficial, 158
  as breach of contract, 160
  compromise view of, 161–163
Corporate taxation, and foreign direct
  investment, 121
Current account
  increase in deficit of U.S., 92n4
  U.S., 36, *37*
Current account deficit
  compared with U.S. economy, 182
  and lag in financial effects, 187
  as share of national income, 182–183
Day of Reckoning, The (B. Friedman), 63
Debt, as percentage of GNP, *148*
Debt Laffer curve, 149, 149n12
Debt policy, need for, 144–145
Debt reduction
  costs of, 150–151
  strategy for, 146, 148–151
Democrats, on budget deficit, 63–64
Deregulation, of savings and loan in-
  dustry, 135–136, 138
Devaluation, 45

Diminished expectations, age of, 4
Direct investment, British vs. Japanese,122–123
Disinflation, costs of, 55–58
Dis-saving, 68
Dixit, Avinash, 109n8
Dollar, 89–100
  compared to Britsh pound, 52
  decline of, 96–98, 133
  depreciation of, 99–100
  effects of decline of, 187–188
  fluctuations in level of, 44
  international role of, 183–185
  purpose of policy on, 89–90
  trend vs. actual value of, 98
Dollar policy, 93–96
Domestic demand, reducing, 49–50
Drexel Burnham Lambert, 158

Economic landscape, 7–27
Economic nationalism
  effects of, 194, 195, 196
  increase of in U.S., 186
Economic structure, Japan's, 119
Economic welfare, roots of, 7–8
Economics, kinds of writing in, ix
Efficiency gains, in takeovers/LBOs, 157–159
Eisner, Robert, 93n5
  on budget deficit, 69–71
  on fear of inflation, 59
Employment
  growth in, 28
  and unemployment, 27–34
Energy crisis, and productivity slowdown, 13
Energy policy, 34
Environmental economics, 34
Equity, and corporate debt, 156
Europe
  as trading bloc, 194
  unemployment rates in, 32
  "Eurosclerosis," 30
Exchange rate(s)
  as mechanism, 46
  nominal vs. real, 94
  and trade, 44
Exporters, and free trade, 102
Exports
  Europe/Japan/U.S., 193
  rate of growth of U.S., 96
  See also Trade
Falling expectations, revolution of, 4
Fallows, James, 109–110

Families, percentage of below poverty level, 3
  See also Median family income
Federal expenditure, comparison of (1987), 75
Federal Reserve Board, 38, 79–87
  and control of economy, 80–81
  and control of inflation, 46–47
  and loss of foreign confidence, 186–187
  and monetarism, 83–84
  and 1929/1987 stock market crashes, 178–179
  and planned recession, 58
  on price stability, 59
  risks to, 85–87
Feldstein, Martin
  on budget deficits, 42
  on flaws in tax system, 108
Financial markets, in 1980s, 133–134
Financing
  vs. forgiving, 145–148
  shift in, 154
Flexible freeze, 76
Foreign direct investment, and corporate taxation, 121
Foreign financing, U.S. prospects for, 182–186
  See also Financing
Foreign-owned firms, share of, 124
Foreign ownership, of U.S. firms, 193
Foreign trade policy, and dollar depreciation, 95
Fortune, xi, 153, 197,
Free trade
  advocates for, 102
  defense of, 104, 106
  as general policy, 112
  and protectionism, 101–113
Frictional unemployment, 32, 38
Friedman, Benjamin, 63
  on risk of financial crisis, 167
Friedman, Milton
  on Federal Reserve, 82, 85
  on natural rate of unemployment, 29
FSLIC (Federal Savings and Loan Insurance Corporation), 136
  and S&L scandal, 137

GATT (General Agreement of Tariffs and Trade), 102n6
Geography, and trade differences, 119
Glenn, Sen. John, 111
GNP (gross national product), 57

money and growth in, *86*
ratio of government debt to, *65*
trend vs. actual, *57*
Gold bugs, 82
Gold standard, 82n3
return to, 44
Great Depression, and protectionism, 103
Greek-letter writing, *ix*
Greenmail, 163
Gross national product. *See* GNP
Grossman, Sanford, 163–164

Hart, Oliver, 163–164
Helpman, Elhanan, 109n8
HIC (highly indebted countries), 143–144
debt as percentage of GNP for, *148*
growth and inflation in, *146*
secondary market for debt of, *150*
Hyperinflation, 52–53

IMF. *See* International Monetary Fund
Import quotas, 132
Imports
Germany's, 118
Japan's, 117, 119
rate of growth of U.S., *96*
See also Trade
Income, changes in real, *21*
Income distribution, 19–26
inequality in, 22
in metropolitan areas, 20
Industrial policy, 15–16, 17
Inflation, 51–60
acceleration of in 1960s, 81
bias toward higher, 193
and business decisions, 53
costs of, 52–54
effects of, 133–134
forecast for, 192–193
and NAIRU, 56
as neutral, 52
and productivity growth, 7
and S&L scandal, 136–137
stabilization of, 51
and tax system, 52
and unemployment, 28, *31*
Inflation rate, in 1980s, 2
Insider trading
concern over, 163, 165
as damaging, 166
Institute for International Economics,

98, 181
Institutional Investor, 186
International competitiveness, of U.S. industry, 44
International economic integration, trend of growing, 194
International economics
new, 109n8
traditional, 109
International economy, forecast for, 193–196
International Monetary Fund (IMF), 93
and Third World debt, 148
International trade
decline in, *195*
rethinking principles of, 108–109

Japan, 115–132
bashers, 116, 119, 119n11
composition of investment flow of, *123*
direct investment of in U.S., 122–127
economic structure of, 119
trade surpluses of, *118*
Japan, Inc., 120
Japanese difference, 116–122
as problem, 128–129
Japanese-owned firms, compared to U.S., 125, *126*, 127
See also Foreign ownership
Jensen, Michael, 155
on corporate takeovers/LBOs, 157–159, 167, 173
Jobs, and trade deficit, 37–39
See also Employment; Unemployment
Jobs, Steve, 153
Junk bond finance, risks of, 167

Kahn, Herman, 197
Kapor, Mitch, 153
Kemp, Rep. Jack, 82
Keynes, John Maynard, 82
Kohlberg Kravis Roberts, 153, 160
Kravis, Henry, 153
Krugman, Paul, 109n8
Kuttner, Robert, 44, 46
on dollar depreciation, 95, 99
on managed trade, 108
trade policy of, 111

Laffer, Arthur, 16
Latin America
debt crisis in, 183, 185, 187

Latin America (cont.)
  trade deficits in, 90–91
Lawrence, Robert, 119n11
LBOs (leveraged buyouts), 154, 154n15
  and corporate debt, 155
Leninism, collapse of, 75n2
Limited industrial policy, purpose of,
  131
Litan, Robert, 137
Living standards, and productivity, 9–10
Losing Ground (Murray), 25
Love in the Ruins (Percy), 197

Macroeconomics of crisis, 186–189
Mainstream, forecast of, 87
Managed trade, 108
  advocates of, 111
  and import quotas, 131–132
Manufactures surplus, Japan's, 117
Market access, as reciprocals, 113
Marris, Stephen, 181
McKinnon, Ronald, 44, 94
Median family income
  forecast for, 192
  in 1980s, 3
  and productivity, 11
  See also Take-home pay
Milken, Michael, 158, 165, 167, 173
Ministry of Finance (Japan), 119, 120
MITI (Ministry of International Trade
  and Industry), 119, 120
Monetarism, Federal Reserve and, 83–84
Monetarists, 82, 85
Monetary aggregates, 82n3
Money, vs. GNP growth, 86
Multi-Fiber Arrangement, 108
Multiplier effect, base money and, 80
Mundell, Robert, 82, 94
Murray, Charles, 25

NAIRU, 29–32
  defined, 29
  forecast for, 192
  and inflation, 56
National income, share of trade in, 195
National savings, 65–69
  and budget deficit, 68–69
  measurement of rate of, 66
  as percent of income, 66–67
  rates of, 70
  and S&L bailout, 141
  and trade deficits, 46–47
Natural rate, of unemployment, 29

Negative saving, 68
Net debtor, U.S. as, 41
Net equity issues, and corporate debt,
  156
Net foreign investment, decline in, 67–68
Net international investment, U.S.,
  39, 40
Net rate of issue of equity, negative, 155
New international economics, 109n8
1929 stock market crash, and 1987's,
  178–179
1987 stock market crash, 133
1988 Trade Act, 36
Nixon, Pres. Richard, 81
Nondefense spending, and budget
  defcit, 74–75

Oil crisis, in U.S., 187
Output gap, 57
Overseas investments, 193
  See also Foreign direct investment,
  Foreign-owned firms, Foreign own-
  ership

Pac-Man defense, 163
Peace dividend, 75n2
Per capita consumption, rise in, 10–12
Percy, Walker, 197
Poison pills, 163
Policy, defined, 62
Poverty
  growth of, 192
  increase in, 20
  War on, 24
Poverty level, percentage of families
  below, 3
Predator's Ball, 158
Prestowitz, Clyde, 111
  on dollar depreciation, 99
  on impact of Japanese-owned firms,
  126, 128
Price stability, as goal, 59
Productivity
  and living standards, 9–10
  and median income, 11
  revival of, 171–173
  and shifts in national power, 12
  slowdown, 13
Productivity boom, consequences of,
  173–175

Productivity growth, 9–17
  rates of, *14*
  results of rapid, 174–175
  U.S., *12*
Protection
  as bargaining threat, 106
  economic case for, 108–112
  and trade deficit, 106–108
Protectionism
  evils of, 103–106
  and free trade, 101–113
  and Great Depression, 103
  politics of, 101–103
  prospect for, 112–113
Protectionist policy, effects of, 49

Rational expectations, decline of, 83
Raw material markets, and decline in
    dollar, 188
Reagan, Pres. Ronald, 33
  conservative economic program of, 135
  on strength of U.S. dollar, 89
  and supply-siders, 16
Recession, 79–82
  as deliberate, 19
  1979–82 as planned, 58
Reich, Robert, 15–16
  on impact of Japanese-owned firms,
    126
Republicans, on budget deficit, 63–64
Rethinking International Trade (Krugman),
    109n8
Rice policy, Japan's, 117n10
Rich, increase in number of, 20, 23
Risk arbitrage, 163, 165
  assessment of, 166
RJR Nabisco, 160
Robber barons, 153–154
Roehm, Carolyne, 13
Roosevelt, Pres. Franklin D., 33

Sachs, Jeffrey, 149n12
  on LDC debt, 185
Sacrifice ratio, 56
Samuelson, Paul, 106
Savings
  decline in rate of U.S., 43
  defined, 65–66
  See also National savings
Savings and loan bailout, cost of to tax-
    payers, 104
Savings and loan industry
  aggressiveness of, 140

  deregulation of, 135–136, 138
  plays double or nothing, 137–140
Savings and loan problem; preventing;
    140–141
Savings and loan scandal, 135–141
  blame for, 139
Sawhill, Isabel, 23
Saxonhouse, Gary, 119
Shleifer, Andrei, 156, 159–161
Shilling, Gary, 115, 194
Smokestack America
  decline in, 24
  downsizing, 162
Smoot-Hawley tariff, 103
Solow, Robert, 14
Solvency, measure of, 64
Spencer, Barbara, 109n8
Stein, Herbert, 39
  on free trade, 129–130
  on trade deficit, 59, 90
Strategic trade policy
  major players engaged in, 112–113
  and subsidies, 110–111
*Strategic Trade Policy and the New Interna-
    tional Economics* (ed. Krugman),
    109n8
Structural impediments, 107n7
Subsidies
  and strategic trade policy, 110–111
  as temporary, 110
Summers, Lawrence, 156, 159–161
Supply-siders, 16
Surpluses, West German
  vs. Japanese, *118*
Switching, and trade deficit, 48

Take-home pay, as stagnant, 1
  See also Median family income
Takeovers
  and corporate debt, 155
  and LBOs, 154, 154n15
Tax reform of 1986, and foreign direct
    investment, 121
Tax system, and inflation, 52
Third World debt, 143–151
  and government intervention, 144–145
Thirtysomething theory, 14
Thurow, Lester, 15–16
"Tory wets," 16
Trade, share of in national income, 195
  See also Exports, Imports
Trade conflict, costs of, 105

Trade deficit, 35–50
  correction of, 90–91
  cost of, 39–40
  emergence of, 35–36
  increase in U.S., *39*
  and jobs, 37–39
  and national savings, 46–47
  and productivity growth, 174
  protection and, 106–108
  reasons for, 42–47
  reducing, 48–50, 90–93
  risks of, 41–42
  solution to, 48
  why worry about, 36–42
Trade restrictions, growth in, 194
Trade surpluses, 117–*118*
Trading blocs, formation of, 194
Trading Places (Prestowitz), 119–120
Trend output, 56, *57*
Twin deficit story, 42–43

Underclass, 22–23
Underlying rate, 55
Unemployment
  and employment, 27–34
  forecast for, 192
  frictional, 32, 38
  meaning of, 27
Unemployment rate
  and inflation, 28, *31*
  in 1980s, *2*
United States
  bilateral trade, *120*
  current account, 36, *37*
  debt crisis fantasy, 179–182
  decline in net foreign investment, 67–68
  domestic economy of, 191–193
  increase in current account deficit, 92n4
  international competitiveness of indus-
    try of, 44
  1990s economic growth, 192
  oil crisis in, 187
  productivity growth in, *12*
  prospects for, 169–170
  rates of export/import growth, *96*
  total trade vs. GNP, *195*
Up-and-down economics, *ix*
Urban Institute, 23
Uruguay Round, 102n6
U.S. Department of Commerce, and
U.S. net international investment position, 40

Venables, Anthony, 112
Volcker, Paul, 58, 83–84

Wall Street Journal, 85
  on dollar policy, 94
Wanniski, Jude, 16, 94
War on Poverty, 24–25
Washington Post, x
Wealth, source of, 154–156
West Germany, trade surpluses of, *118*
White knights, 163
Wolfe, Tom, 19
Wolferen, Karel van, 120
World Bank, and Third World debt, 148
Wriston, Walter, 143

Year 2000, The (Kahn et al.), 197
Yuppie phenomenon, 23